James Evans: Inventor of the Syllabic System of the Cree Language

John MacLean

REV. JAMES EVANS.

JAMES EVANS

INVENTOR OF THE SYLLABIC SYSTEM OF THE CREE LANGUAGE.

BY

JOHN McLEAN, M.A., PH.D.,

(ROBIN RUSTLER).

Author of "The Indians of Canada: Their Manners and Customs," etc., etc.

TORONTO:
METHODIST MISSION ROOMS.
1890.

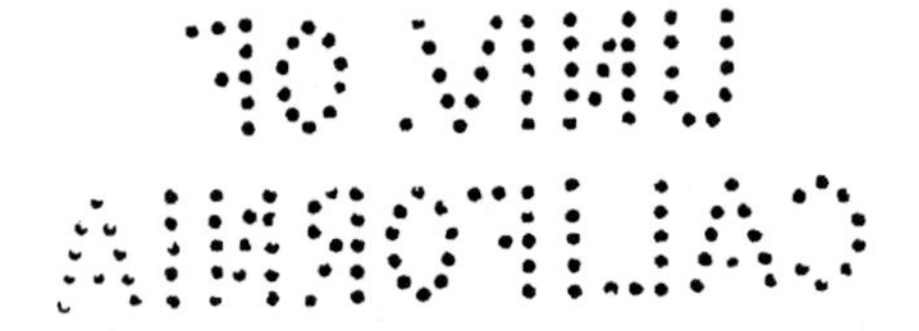

TO THE MEMORY OF

The Men and Women

WHO HAVE NOBLY TOILED AMONG

THE INDIAN TRIBES OF THE GREAT NORTH-WEST

THIS BOOK IS AFFECTIONATELY DEDICATED.

PREFACE.

LONG did we wait for a short biography of the man who did so much for the Indian tribes of the great North-West, but it came not. Much thought upon our negligence in not doing something to remind the Christian public of the heroism of a brave Canadian Missionary, caused me to assume the responsibility, although other minds and hearts could have done better in inditing a life so full of devotion and courage. In the midst of other duties these pages have been written, a few at a time, with repeated interruptions. I hope that all the imperfections will be overlooked in the sincere desire to do something that may prove helpful to young and old, and to discharge a duty incumbent upon all friends of Canadian Missions, and more especially those belonging to the Methodist Church.

JOHN McLEAN.

MOOSEJAW, ASSINIBOIA,
March 10th, 1890.

CONTENTS.

CHAPTER VIII.

CHAPTER IX.

CHAPTER X.

CHAPTER XI.

CHAPTER XII.

CHAPTER XIII.

LIST OF ILLUSTRATIONS.

THE RED RIVER VOYAGEUR.

Out and in the river is winding
  The links of its long, red chain
Through belts of dusky pine-land
  And gusty leagues of plain.

Only, at times, a smoke-wreath
  With the drifting cloud-rack joins,
The smoke of the hunting-lodges
  Of the wild Assiniboins!

Drearily blows the north-wind
  From the land of ice and snow;
The eyes that look are weary,
  And heavy the hands that row.

And with one foot on the water,
  And one upon the shore,
The Angel of Shadow gives warning
  That day shall be no more.

Is it the clang of wild-geese?
  Is it the Indian's yell
That lends to the voice of the north-wind
  The tones of a far-off bell?

The voyageur smiles as he listens
  To the sound that grows apace;
Well he knows the vesper ringing
  Of the bells of St. Boniface.

The bells of the Roman Mission,
  That call from their turrets twain,
To the boatman on the river,
  To the hunter on the plain!

Even so, in our mortal journey
  The bitter north-winds blow,
And thus upon life's Red River
  Our hearts, as oarsmen, row.

And when the Angel of Shadow
  Rests his feet on wave and shore,
And our eyes grow dim with watching,
  And our hearts faint at the oar.

Happy is he who heareth
  The signal of his release
In the bells of the Holy City,
  The chimes of eternal peace!

— *Whittier*.

JAMES EVANS,

THE CANADIAN CADMUS.

CHAPTER I.

PARENTAGE AND YOUTH.

MASTER missionaries are born, not made. Genius belongs not solely to the ranks of literature, science and art; but in the lower paths of life there walk amongst us men worthy to rule by right, who leave the impress of their thought upon the hearts of their fellows, ever increasing in its productive power, until it is recovered upon the other side of life.

Literature, science and art may be called the higher walks of life, but they are only so if they lead to nobler living; while the loftier paths are those that direct to purity of life and development of character, and of these none can boast of greater devotion, purer thinking and living, and holier aims, than that of missions. A missionary genius is worthy our most enthusiastic study and admiration, for the con-

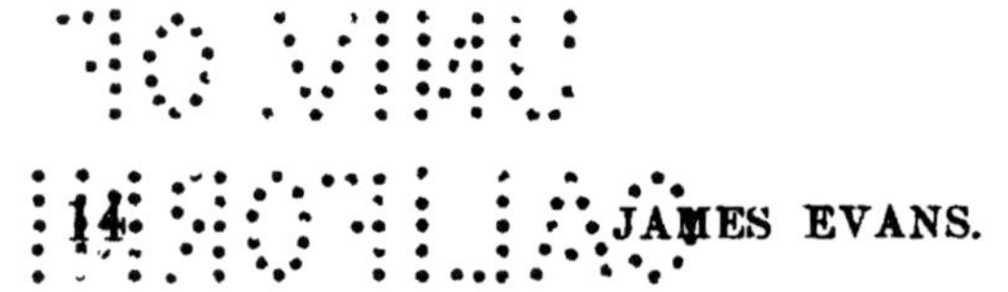

templation of such a life is fraught with good. Not the life of a missionary merely, are we studying, but that of a philologist, inventor, explorer and patriot, whose noblest ambition was to live for his country, humanity and God.

James Evans was born in Kingston-upon-Hull, England, on the eighteenth day of January, in the year eighteen hundred and one. His father was a sailor, and sailed in the year eighteen hundred as master of a merchant vessel for Cronstadt, a Russian port in the Baltic, and during his absence James was born. There was trouble in Russia, and war was expected to be declared against England, an embargo having been laid upon all British vessels, and the crews taken into the interior of the country; so Mary Evans, the mother of James, felt afraid that her husband would never return. The parents of the child were Wesleyan Methodists, and the Christian mother took her babe to the Carthruse Methodist Church in Hull, where he was christened James, after his godly father in the land of the Czar. The Emperor Paul having been assassinated, the embargo was taken off the British vessels, and the sailors returned to their island home, amongst the number being Captain James Evans, who was joyously welcomed by his wife, and the happy father rejoiced in his infant boy. The boy grew up buoyant in spirits, honest, fearless and intelligent, with a strong desire to follow his father's calling and live at home upon the sea. The smell of the salt water had great attractions for him, and when only eight years of age he was a good swimmer, evidently equipped for the hardships and daring of an old salt. The sea-captain did not entertain the same opinions as the youth, and determined to destroy his foolish desires by taking him to sea, that he might prove the folly of his choice. When only eight years of age, he was taken by his father upon two voyages, one to Dantzic, and the other to Copenhagen. He was subjected to very hard fare during these trial trips, and whether or not they had the desired effect, at any rate he was not destined to be a sailor, although the lessons learned at this time proved to be of great service to him in after life, as he labored amongst the Indian tribes in the Dominion.

His father took command of a transport and troopship named the *Triton*, and sailed for the Mediterranean, where the mother of James and his youngest brother joined the ship. James and his brother Ephraim—now the Rev. Dr. Ephraim Evans, of London, Ontario—were sent to a boarding school in Lincolnshire, to continue their studies during the absence of their parents, and at this school James remained until he was fifteen years old.

He was afterwards apprenticed to a grocer, that he

might learn the trade, and with his employer he boarded during his short apprenticeship. His employer was an office-bearer in the Wesleyan Methodist Church, and he had, therefore, an opportunity of attending all the services, besides being expected to do so.

The famous Gideon Ouseley, the Irish missionary of evangelistic renown, was at this time travelling through England, preaching and lecturing on behalf of the Irish Churches under his care; and wherever he went he not only collected funds, but won souls for his Master. James Evans, attracted by the fame of this mighty preacher of righteousness, listened to the truth as it fell from his lips, and was smitten with sorrow. The saddened heart soon arose from the dust, for the joys of the Calvary cross and the glory of the celestial land streamed gently down upon him, and he sang with quivering lip and glowing faith,

"My God is reconciled,
His pardoning voice I hear,
He owns me for His child,
I can no longer fear.
With confidence I now draw nigh,
And Father, Abba, Father, cry."

It was Dr. Chalmers, the eminent Presbyterian divine, who said that "Methodism is Christianity in earnest;" and true to her origin and doctrines, the young convert was taught how to work, by lisping tongue and gentle life. He was placed on the "plan" among the prayer-leaders, and initiated into the band of earnest toilers who have done so much in the Old World and the New to introduce and maintain the polity and power of the Methodist Church. Shortly afterward he was drafted into the ranks of the faithful men—the local preachers—who sang and prayed with loosened tongues,

> "Happy if with my latest breath
> I may but speak His name,
> Preach Him to all, and cry in death,
> Behold! behold the Lamb!"

Such a happy life and such training failed not to bring their reward in the development of the powers, intellectual and spiritual, of the young man; and in a short space of time he was preaching earnest and acceptable sermons to the dwellers in the towns and villages around his home.

The Evans family emigrated to Canada, and settled at Lachute, in the Province of Quebec. James was at this time engaged in a large glass and crockery establishment in London, and came not with the family, but remained for about the space of two years, and then came to Canada, where he joined his parents and friends in their new home.

City life to a young man is fraught with many

INDIAN'S SUMMER DRESS.

temptations, especially directed against a life of earnest religion; and during the years spent in London the young convert lost his quickened interest and holy zeal in matters relating to the heart and life, so that he no longer claimed his position as a member of the Methodist Church. His love for the Church itself was not, however, quenched, as he admired her doctrines and polity, and believed in all the fundamental truths of our common Christianity.

A few months after his arrival in Canada he began the profession of school-teaching, which, in those days, had not become so fully developed as to be worthy the name of a profession in the colony. Knowledge sufficient for his pupils and aptitude to teach were all that were needed to secure a position. The rigid examinations of Boards of Examiners, Normal training, and certificates from Boards of Education were unnecessary things for the young teacher, who had oftentimes to "board around" amongst the parents of his pupils, and engage in "odd kinds of work," in order that he might eke out an existence. A school was soon opened near L'Orignal, where young Evans taught, and during this period of intellectual life and labor, he became susceptible to the gentler influences of love. It was here that he met Miss Mary Blithe Smith, and was charmed by her attractions. The friendship thus begun soon ripened into love, and the marriage was consummated about 1823. Life was freighted with responsibilities that aforetime he knew nothing of, but the new relation into which he had entered secured for him a companion of his joys and sorrows, a worthy fellow burden bearer, and one well qualified for all the serious duties of a missionary life, upon which very soon both should enter. Two years of married life were spent in Lower Canada, and then, about the year 1825, they removed to Upper Canada, guided by the hand of Providence to spheres of usefulness, where they unitedly might receive inspiration for earnest, holy toil, by hearing the voice of the Man of Nazareth calling them from sin and world-likeness to lives of intense devotion to God and man. Apparently drifting westward, yet certainly guided in a definite course, they settled in their new home, and not long afterwards a camp-meeting was held at Augusta, which they attended, and there James Evans felt anew the kindlings of God's love. The consecration of the physical, intellectual and spiritual natures of the man was complete; the baptism of the Spirit gave full attestation of the acceptation of the sacrifice, and immediately there arose duties and responsibilities, aspirations and aims, which filled his life with a deeper sacredness and a holier meaning, and the joy of doing good became his hope and reward. His wife bowed at the altar of mercy, seeking pardon and purity, and as she wept at the Cross of the Crucified, the Master smiled and gently sent her on her way, rejoicing in the consciousness of sins forgiven.

Husband and wife were henceforth partners in one glorious hope, united in a common cause, toiling together for the weal of humanity, and ever striving with all their consecrated powers to lead men into paths of usefulness, where God would be their guide and friend. The great Master of life was preparing them for their life-work, by the impartation of a new affection, and the imposing of a burden for soul-saving upon their hearts. Young, ardent and hopeful, their hearts filled with love to God and man, they were well adapted to win souls for Christ, and to lead that others might follow them in the paths of truth and peace.

CHAPTER II.

THE CANADIAN ABORIGINES.

THE native Canadians were a numerous people when Jacques Cartier and his French courtiers were visited upon Canadian soil by Donnacona, the Lord of Canada, and in the simplicity and honesty of the forest red man, they accepted without fear the hospitality of their brother in white. The bold and warlike Iroquois first listened to the sound of the Gospel from the lips of the Jesuit missionaries, who followed them from camp to camp, dreading not the hardships of the journey, the privations of savage life, or the warrior's scalping-knife, if only they might baptize a few children or win some of their dusky friends into the path of light. Brebeuf and Jogues led the way through martyrdom into the homes and hearts of the savage tribes, and with cross and rosary, enthusiastic men followed, counting not their lives dear, that they might enjoy the opportunity of pointing the dying warrior to the Christ of Calvary. The French occupation of Canada gave the Jesuits the first opportunity, which they embraced, of preaching to the Indians. The fall of Quebec, and the subsequent events of that period, prepared the way for the evangelization of the tribes inhabiting Ontario, western and north-western Canada. There were living in western Canada bands and tribes belonging to the Lenni-Lenape, Algonquin, and Iroquois confederacies, who had never seen a missionary or heard the sound of Jesus' name. Chippewa, Mississauga, Oneida, Mohawk, Cayuga, Seneca, Onondaga, Tuscarora, Muncey, Delaware, Shawnee and Pottawatomie Indians dwelt in the forests and along the rivers, worshipping the creatures of their own imagination or following the doctrines taught by their fathers in their native religious system. They painted their bodies in the most grotesque fashion, kept up their religious festivals, danced at their feasts in accordance with their marriage, war or social customs, and thought little of the morrow. Every crag, rapid, or strangely shaped tree had its familiar spirit, which haunted the spot and demanded a sacrifice. Superstition filled the hearts of the people with fear, and through war, jealousy, famine, disease and superstitious dread, they seldom enjoyed peace, and placid, permanent joy was a stranger to the wigwam or lodge of the red man. At the beginning of the present century, Methodism was seeking a resting-place in Canada, and occasionally the preacher, with his saddle-bags, made his appearance, stopping at the door of the small log cabin, seeking a congregation, addressing the master of the habitation in a straightforward manner, "I have come to talk to you about religion, and to pray with you. If you are willing to receive me for this purpose, I will stop; if not, I will go on." The men who visited these humble dwellings in the interests of religion were shrewd and intelligent, and in not a few instances educated and refined. Inspired by the love of God, and yearning for the salvation of their fellows, they left the college campus, with all its hallowed associations; the homes of their childhood, so full of endearing memories; the populated village, town or city, with the refining influences of cultured society, and into the wilds of the west they went, happy in the consciousness of sins forgiven, preaching Christ the crucified, and a hope of heaven.

Happy days were these, so full of hardship and toil, but blessed in results. One of the most notable of the early Methodist preachers who visited Canada, and spent some years there, was Nathan Bangs, whose memory is precious to all Methodists in Canada, and is treasured in the literature of United States Methodism. He came as a young surveyor in 1799 to Canada to practise his profession, and whilst living with his pious sister and her husband, he gave his life to God. He was sent out to preach in 1802, remained a few years in the country, returned to the United States, held important positions in the Church, and became honored in literature as the historian of Methodism.

Mr. Bangs passed through some strange experiences in the country, which he afterwards related with much zest. On his way to one of his preaching places, he was detained by a broken bridge and a dangerous creek, so he found shelter in the home of an Indian trader, where a dance was going on. After having danced till near midnight, the people were still determined to continue, but the young preacher was anxious to have them desist, and he tells us the result of his stay in that home in the following language:

"I then said to the chief trader, who had become very friendly with me, 'With your permission I will address a few words to the people.' He assented, and requested them to give attention. I arose and addressed them in substance as follows: 'It is now midnight, and the holy Sabbath is begun. You have amused yourselves with dancing, I think, long enough to satisfy you, if not to fatigue you; and if you continue it any longer you will not only be transgressing the law of God, but likewise the law of your country. I advise you, therefore, to desist, and to retire to rest.' They complied so far as to cease dancing. But the Indian trader came to me and said, 'The Indians are encamped a short distance from us, and they expect a dance here, as I have promised them one.' He asked my permission to let them have it. I replied I had no control over his house or the Indians, but if he would dispense with the revel he would highly gratify me, and, I doubted not, please God. He rejoined that, as he had promised them the dance, they would expect

INDIAN OF THE CAMP.

it. He then went to the door, and gave the Indian whoop, and down came the savages and began an Indian dance, which, with their drumming on an old pan, their frequent yells, their stamping and bodily distortions, presented a spectacle fit for pandemonium.

I requested the trader to assist me in conversing with them. To this he assented, when the chief of the Indians presented himself before me with great dignity and gravity. I asked him if he knew whence he had descended. He replied, "Yes; the Great Spirit at first made one man and one woman, placed them on an island an acre in size; thence they were driven out, for an act of disobedience, to the continent, and from them they were descended." I then gave him an account of the creation of the world, of man in particular, of his fall and its consequences. I asked him if he had ever heard of Jesus Christ. He replied, "No." I then gave him an account of our Lord's birth, His life, miracles and teachings, His sufferings and death. While describing the death of Christ, the chief pointed to his heart and lifted his eyes and hands towards heaven, apparently filled with amazement. When I had concluded, he clasped me in his arms, kissed me, and called me father, and entreated me to come and live with him and be the teacher of his people. After assuring him of my affection for them, and the deep interest I felt in their eternal welfare, I told him that I could not comply with his request, but that the time was not far distant when a Christian teacher should be sent to them. They then retired to their encampment. But the worst of this strange night was still to come. There were two traders present, one of whom, the head man, had become intoxicated, and still wanted more liquor. The other refused to let him have it. The dispute ran high, and the drunken trader raised his fist to strike the other, when I stepped in and arrested the blow. He then swore that if he was not allowed more whiskey, he would call the Indians and fall upon and murder us all. He accordingly went to the door, and gave the murderous "whoop," and the Indians came rushing to the house. Meantime, those within armed themselves as well as they could with sticks and clubs, determined to defend themselves to the utmost. I shuddered for the consequences. The enraged man then said, "Here are my guards at the door; if you will give me more whiskey, well; if you will not, they shall fall upon you, and we will murder you all." "Will you?" the other exclaimed, and lifted his hand to strike him down. I again stepped between them, and placing my hand upon the drunken man's shoulder, said, 'Come, my friend, let us go to sleep. If you will be my friend, I will be yours.' He consented. We laid down upon a bed, and in a few minutes he was asleep. I then arose. The Indians had retired to their camp, and at dawn I started on my way, persuading two men to accompany me to the creek and help me over by laying logs on the broken bridge. I passed on, praising God for delivering me from the perils of this dismal night, and for enabling me to prevent the shedding of blood, as well as for the pleasing interview I had with the Indian chief."

The interest manifested by Dr. Bangs, when a young man, in the native tribes of Canada, continued throughout his scholarly life after his departure to the United States, and upon several occasions was he able to render very efficient and acceptable help to the missionaries laboring for the elevation of the Red Race. In the early years of the present century there was little interest shown in the religious welfare of the Indians of Ontario, and the scientific study of the literature, languages and customs of the Indians had not yet begun. Occasionally a traveller, more observant than his fellows, noticed the marks of native culture in the relics of the people, and being favorably impressed with what he saw, wrote for the benefit of others the results of his study and travel. One of these studious travellers was the Rev. Dr. Reed, whose records illustrative of Canadian Indian life are worthy of perusal and preservation. "At the head of Lake Ontario there is a considerable body of water, separated from the lake by a sandy beach about five miles in length, and from eighty to one hundred yards in width. The water thus separated from the lake is called Burlington Bay, at the upper end of which now stands the city of Hamilton. The outlet of the bay into the lake is near the north end of the beach, and is celebrated as a famous fishing place. The Indians have some curious traditions concerning this particular region, to which I will presently refer. I noticed, in passing over this beach, singular excavations at regular intervals about midway between the lake and the bay. They were about twenty or thirty rods apart, originally of a square form, and measuring from ten to fifteen yards on a side. They were evidently artificial, and of a very ancient date, as in some instances old trees were growing within them, and the Indians had no tradition of their origin or design. I judge that they must have been intended for military use. At the north end of the beach, on the main land, beautifully situated near the lake shore, was the elegant residence of Colonel Brant, son of the old chief of revolutionary celebrity. The Colonel was an educated and well-bred gentleman, and with his family associated with the higher classes of society. In this immediate vicinity the soil was mingled with vast quantities of human bones, stones, arrow-heads, hatchets, etc., the weapons of ancient Indian warfare. In sight of the mansion, and in plain view of the road, was a large mound of earth filled with human bones. One or two others stood near, but had been demolished. In several instances, I was informed, stone hatchets and arrow-heads had been found firmly fixed in skulls, plainly indicating that the victims had fallen in some hostile encounter.

The Indian traditions respecting these bones is as follows: "The Chippewas once had undivided possession of this region of country, and for many years enjoyed the monopoly of its fine hunting grounds and fishing places. The Mohawks on the east of the lakes, in what is now Western New York, had long coveted this territory, and finally resolved upon an attempt to conquer it and dispossess its rightful owners. Accordingly they crossed the Niagara River, marched up the lake to the bay, fought their way across the beach, and on the main land, where now lay the bones of slaughtered thousands, fought a long, terrible, and final battle.

"The Mohawks say they defeated and scattered the Chippewas; and, among the rest, the Rev. John Sunday, a chief of that nation, says that they successfully repelled the Mohawk invasion. And this version is supported by their keeping possession of the grounds, the Mohawks of the Grand River being deported to this country by the British Government, at the close of the Revolutionary War, and not originally indigenous to the soil."

Dr. Reed was not versed in Indian lore, and consequently was unable to give accurately, in detail, the records of traditional battles, migrations and customs, still these jottings reveal the occasional sympathetic student, anxious to aid the Indians, the man of science and the missionary in his toil. There were some persons interested in the aborigines, but it was a matter of pecuniary self-interest. The native hunters and trappers had furs to sell, and they required some of the necessaries of life, so traders were induced to go amongst the tribes buying and selling, and invariably making their homes with them. The traders were generally men of small capital, who saw that they could easily make money through a system of Indian merchandise. Accordingly, they purchased a small supply of goods, amongst which were generally some kegs of whiskey, and proceeding to the Indian camp they carried on their "trades" by means of barter. Some of these traders visited these camps at stated periods and then left, but others built houses, lived with the Indians, and marrying some of the dusky maidens, spent their lives in the vicinity of the camps. Sometimes there were found men of intelligence, descended from an ancient and honorable stock, acting as Indian traders. Lured by the hope of gain, or thrown by fickle fortune upon the mercies of a cold and cruel world, they had drifted toward the red man's refuge. In general, the life of an Indian trader was one of debauchery, immorality and pain. Whiskey demoralized the Indians, and the trader then took advantage of them to increase his wealth by fair means or foul. A few of the traders engaged in their business in an honorable way, refusing to sell whiskey, and seeking to deal honestly; they felt that the natives had souls, and were entitled to respect and love.

HALF-BREED.

The settlements of the white people in the country being new, and the settlers poor, the ministers who carried the Gospel to them were compelled to live on scanty fare, dress in the plainest fashion, ride long distances between the preaching places, and perform missionary toil, as difficult, and more uninviting than is be found in China, India, Africa or Japan. There were severe hardships, and small salary, hard work and little rest. The days of Indian missions had not arrived, for the ministers were few, and all their time was fully occupied with the missions to the white people. The Indians might attend the services held on these missions, but they seldom understood the language of the descendants of the white conquerors, and they felt their inferior position, arising from drunkenness, disease and poverty, so they sought not the teachings of the Nazarene. The Man of Nazareth was nothing to them, believing as they did and cherishing deeply their native religion. Lack of men and funds prevented anything being done on their behalf, but there were many persons interested in their welfare, temporal and spiritual, who sought to help them toward a better life. About the year eighteen hundred and twenty, there arose a keen and abiding manifeststion of sympathy and love toward these neglected children of the forest, which was felt in the Christian communities and ultimately resulted in the organization of missions and schools. The Rev. William Case had been touched by the wretchedness which he witnessed in the Indian camps, as he rode to the white settlements, and he desired earnestly to lead these people in the way of peace and light and truth. The desire begotten in his breast increased, until it burned as the ruling passion of his life for thirty years. He became the presiding genius of the Indian work in the country, the Canadian Apostle of the Indians, seeking and finding men and money for sending the Gospel to these people, training teachers and preachers, educating the Indian youth, superintending translations of hymns, portions of the Bible, and other kinds of literature, and caring for the manual training of the Indians. It was he who discovered and trained James Evans, inventor of the Cree Syllabic system; George McDougall, the missionary martyr of the Saskatchewan; Henry B. Steinhauer, who translated the greater part of the Bible into the Cree language, Kahkewayquonaby—Peter Jones—native preacher, translator and author; Shawundais—John Sunday—the Indian chief, orator and missionary, and a host of others who have devoted time, energy, talent and wealth for the salvation of the Indian race. Christianize and then civilize the Indians, was his motto. Still he did not perform mission work and neglect the civilization, for he toiled amid innumerable difficulties that he might teach the people the art of self-support, and on his mission at Alderville, the Manual Labor School was part of the religious life of the Indian youth. Dr. Reed mentions an instance of Case's work amongst the Indians before the era of Indian missions in Upper Canada had dawned. "An instance of the happy illustration of the truth: he was preaching once to a company of Indians, and endeavoring to impress them with the idea of the great love of God in giving His Son to die for the world. They shook their heads and murmured their dislike of the idea that an innocent being should be made to die for the guilty. Perceiving this, he related to them the story of Pocahontas and Captain Smith, of which they had traditional knowledge. He told them how the king's daughter threw herself upon the body of the victim whom her father had abandoned to death, and declared they might kill her, but they must not kill the white man, and thus, for her sake, his life was saved. Immediately the Indians showed the most lively and intense interest, and seemed to comprehend and approve the plan of salvation by the death of Christ." The enthusiasm existing in the breasts of a few men in the work of Christianizing the Indians rapidly spread, and the scattered bands heard with joy the good news of salvation through the Great Master of Life, Jesus Christ.

CHAPTER III.

BEGINNINGS OF INDIAN MISSIONS.

CANADIAN Protestant Indian Missions began about the year eighteen hundred and twenty. Previous to that time David Zeisberger had fled to Canada with his Christian Wyandots and established an Indian mission, which was cared for by this faithful man of God, and his fellow Moravian missionaries, but all other attempts were lacking in organization and failed. A wave of Christian influences seemed to have been borne westward about this period, and blessed results followed.

Roman Catholic Indian mission work originated with Las Casas, whose zeal and love manifested among the Indians in Mexico, begat animosity and strife, and the Spanish conquerors detested the faithful priest who dared to care for the Indians' souls, and confront the selfish interests of his own countrymen. The story of his devotion, sufferings and perseverance have blessed the toilers among men in many lands.

David Zeisberger labored for sixty years as a missionary to the red men, and the records of his life contain grammars, dictionaries, hymn-books, portions of the Scriptures, and books of various kinds, translated or prepared in the Delaware and other Indian languages. John Eliot toiled amid the opposition of the colonists among the Indians, teaching, farming, building, preaching and translating; and strange sensations take possession of us as we gaze upon his translation of the Bible, and learn that there are only eight copies of the book in existence, one scholar alone in the world able to read it, and not a single descendant living of the people for whom this translation was made. David Brainerd spent four successful years amongst the Delawares, and rejoiced in seeing hundreds converted to the Christian faith. John B. Finlay among the Wyandots, and other faithful men in the camps by the rivers, in the forests and upon the prairies, told the story of redeeming love, and the painted savages forsook the scalp-dance and heathen feasts for the forest temple where God was praised. Many of the red men laid aside the scalp-lock, carried the beautiful white wampum belts with the design of the cross neatly inwrought with shells, symbolical of the Christian faith, buried the hatchet, and became teachers of righteousness. In Great Britain, United States and Canada there sprang up, at once in the breasts of Christian people, intense sympathy for the Indians. The missionary zeal spread, and men travelled independently to the camps to tell "the old,

old story" to painted, eager listeners. In the home circle, at social gatherings, and church conferences, the clergy and laity spake of sending the Gospel to the Indians. In Ontario, the English Church and the Methodist Church contemplated sending missionaries to the wigwams; and in the Red River Settlement, westward toward the fertile lands of Manitoba and the North-West Territories, the Rev. John West, in eighteen hundred and twenty, began his labors among the white settlers and Indians. For several years William Case had been seeking to help the Indians, having witnessed the degradation of the Mississaugas around Burlington Bay, and the need of the Six Nations for some power stronger than they possessed to elevate them intellectually and spiritually, being anxious to lead men to God. The report of successful labor among the Wyandots in the United States gave a fresh impetus to his zeal, so that he was ever urging his people to remember in their prayers the native tribes of Canada.

At the Conference held in July, eighteen hundred and twenty-one, William Case and Henry Ryan, with three other gentlemen, were appointed a "Committee on Indian Affairs," and during this year matters had progressed so favorably that an opening was effected for beginning missionary work on a systematic plan. Whilst William Case was meditating upon these things, and urging people to care for the Indians, there went on a visit to the Six Nation Indians at Grand River the Rev. Alvin Torry, who became deeply impressed that something should be done for the spiritual welfare of the people. Torry related the events of his visit to William Case, and mutual was the surprise, for financial help had been promised Case to send a man, and he found the missionary needed in Alvin Torry, who became the first Indian missionary of the Methodist Church in the Dominion. At the same time there went from Saratoga, N.Y., Seth Crawford, a young man anxious to learn the language of the people that he might win their souls for God, and on the Grand River Mission he labored as a school teacher, boarding with the Indians and rejoicing in successful toil.

Among the Six Nation Indians at Grand River there officiated occasionally, in the old Mohawk Church on the Reservation, an English Church clergyman from one of the neighboring settlements, and an Indian chief performed the duties of catechist. The Mohawk Church was the oldest Protestant Church in Ontario. The Grand River Mission, begun by Alvin Torry and Seth Crawford, under the direction of William Case, was the first Methodist Indian Mission in the Dominion. Amongst the first converts of this mission were Peter Jones and his sister Kahkewayquonaby — Peter

Jones—became deeply serious on religious matters, through associating with Seth Crawford and listening to the sermons preached by Alvin Torry, Edmund Stoney, and other preachers of the Gospel. At a camp-meeting held in the township of Ancaster, when William Case requested all who had been converted to stand, Peter Jones and his sister arose; and then, as Elder Case recognized the young man in the group of those standing, he exclaimed, "Glory to God, there stands a son of Augustus Jones, of the Grand River, amongst the converts; now is the door opened for the work of conversion among his nation!" And so it proved, for Peter Jones became a zealous and successful missionary, through whose efforts John Sunday and thousands of Indians belonging to the Ojibway, Six Nation and other Indian tribes were led to Christ. The missionaries to the white settlers visited the Indian camps when their time and pressing duties permitted; but there were so many difficulties connected with Indian missionary work that it seemed hopeless in the beginning. Drunkenness prevailed to such an extent among the tribes, that men of faith and zeal doubted the propriety of engaging in missionary work amongst them. Torry says, that he "was accustomed to cross the Grand River within a few miles of the Mohawk tribe, and frequently met with groups of them here and there, and not unfrequently saw them lying drunk around huckster shops kept by white people for the purpose of getting the Indians drunk, and then robbing them of all that was of use to them. But it had never occurred to me that the Gospel of Christ could be the power of God to the salvation of the Indians." Peter Jones states: "Shortly after this we removed from the head of the lake to the Grand River, and settled among the Mohawk Indians. These people were professedly members of the Church of England, and had an old church—the oldest in the Province—where a number assembled every Sabbath to hear the prayers read by one of the chiefs, named Henry Aaron Hill. They were also visited occasionally by ministers of the Church of England. I regret to state that the Gospel preached among them seemed to have little or no effect upon their moral conduct. In this respect they were no better than their pagan brethren. Drunkenness, quarrelling and fighting were the prevailing vices of the Six Nations of Indians. They were also much given to fiddling and dancing. In all these things, I believe the Mohawks excelled the other tribes." The Indians were deeply attached to their native religion and delighted in the feasts, sacrifices, amulets, and other religious beliefs and customs. Gospel influences, introduced by the missionaries, however, soon wrought decided changes among them, so that in a short time they rejoiced in their new-found joy, and the hearts of the men who had begun to toil amongst them were strangely warmed and encouraged to go on in the path of Indian evangelization.

William Case saw the divine guidance in the work in which he had so earnestly engaged, and he writes to the *Methodist Magazine*, published in New York, on the 27th of August, 1823: "To the friends of Zion it will be a matter of joy to hear that a fine work of religion is progressing among the Indians on Grand River. Last Sabbath several of them attended our quarterly meeting at Long Point, and in love-feast they spoke in an impressive manner of their late conversion, and the exercise of grace on their hearts. One of them said he had been desirous of knowing the way of peace for thirty years, but had not found it till lately Jesus gave him peace. The work is prevailing in the north part of the reservation, where a few of different tribes are settled together. This we think to be a favorable circumstance in the providence of God, for the instruction of the other tribes. Their meetings are powerful, and some overwhelming, and it is a most affecting scene to hear these children of the forest, in their native Mohawk and Mississauga, weeping for their sins, or giving glory to God for redemption through the Saviour. About twelve or fourteen have obtained a joyful hope; some are now

GEORGE McDOUGALL.

under awakening; and others are coming to inquire *what these strange things mean!* Their meetings are remarkably solemn, and they vent their feelings with abundance of tears. Among the converted are men who had long drank the poisonous fire of ardent spirits from the hands of pernicious white men. They are now sober and watchful Christians, taking only 'the cup of salvation, and calling on the name of the Lord.'"

The good work of grace so auspiciously begun continued to grow, until the men forsook the cup and dance, and learned to toil in hope for their daily bread. The women revealed to the world the power and value of the religion of the Christ by cleanlier homes and holier lives. Some very striking instances of conversion took place, notably among the women in the wigwams. Two women became deeply concerned about the salvation of their souls, one of whom had in former years been a happy follower of Christ, but yielding to temptation, she had lost her peace of mind and hope of eternal life. When she found anew the Redeemer of men, she began to toil for souls. The other was a poor sufferer in body, and, added to her personal physical affliction, many heavy trials had befallen her family which had weighed heavily upon her spirit. The happy convert urged her to pray, that relief might come to body and soul. As she went to the spring for water, she turned aside several times to pray, and at last became insensible. Upon recovering, she returned home and earnestly continued her supplications, with her children gathered around her. Her eldest daughter became deeply impressed, and besought pardon upon her knees. Soon she was rejoicing in the possession of that "peace of God which passeth all understanding," and then the youngest, aged four years, began to say to the mother, "Send for the minister." The light soon dawned upon the darkened, weary soul, and joy unspeakable chased the grief away.

Seth Crawford, while laboring among these people at Grand River in 1823, mentions a meeting held on the last Sabbath of July, which was remarkable for its results. "During singing and prayer there was much melting of heart and fervency throughout the assembly. Some trembled and wept, others sunk on the floor, and there was a great cry for mercy throughout the congregation. Some cried in Mississauga, 'Chemenito! Kitta maugesse, chemuch nene,' etc., *i.e.*, 'Great Good Spirit! I am poor and evil,' etc. Others, in Mohawk, prayed, 'Oh Sayaner, souahhaah sadoeyn Roewaye, Jesus Christ, tandakweanderhek,' that is, 'O Lord, the only begotten Son, Jesus Christ, have mercy on us.' Others were encouraging the penitents to cast their burdens on the Lord. Others, again, were rejoicing over their converted friends and converted neighbors. In this manner the meetings continued throughout the day. While these exercises were going on, a little girl ran home to call her mother, who came directly over to the meeting. On entering the room where the people were praying, she was smitten with conviction and fell down, crying for mercy. While in this distress, her husband was troubled lest his wife should die, but was happily disappointed when, a few hours after, her sorrows were turned into joy, and she arose praising the Lord. From this time the husband set out to serve the Lord, and the next day he also found peace to his soul, as I will hereafter relate. During the day several found the Saviour's love, and retired with great peace and comfort; while others, with heavy hearts, wept and prayed as they returned comfortless to their habitations. The next day I visited them, when they welcomed me with much affection, delcaring what peace and happiness they felt since their late conversion. A number soon came together, among whom was the Indian who, the day before, was so concerned for his wife. His convictions for sin appeared deep, and his mind was in much distress. We joined in prayer for him; when I had closed, an Indian woman prayed in Mohawk. While she was, with great earnestness, presenting to the Lord the case of this broken-hearted sinner, the Lord set his soul at liberty. Himself and family have since appeared much devoted to the service of the Lord. The next morning, assisted by an interpreter, I again preached to the Indians. After the meeting, observing a man leaning on the fence weeping; I invited him to a neighboring thicket, where I sung and prayed with him. I then called on him to pray; he began, and cried aloud for mercy with much contrition of spirit; but his tone was soon changed from prayer to praise. The work is spreading into a number of families. Sometimes the parents, sometimes the children, are first brought under concern. Without delay they fly to God by prayer, and generally they do not long mourn before their souls are at liberty. The change which has taken place among these people appears very great, and, I doubt not, will do honor to the cause of religion, and thereby glorify God, who has promised to give the Gentiles for the inheritance of His Son."

The subject of Canadian Indian missions began to attract seriously the attention of Christian people, and at the missionary meetings it was the theme of the ablest speakers. At the first anniversary of the Canada Conference Missionary Society, held on September, 1825, at the Fifty Mile Creek, Peter Jones and others attended the meeting, which was addressed by the eloquent and dignified Mohawk chief, Thomas

Davis. He was an able and useful man, of whom it has been written, "As an orator, he would have graced any of our legislative halls, and he far exceeded many who hold themselves up as patterns in that art." Bishop Hedding listened to his relation of Christian experience in his native Mohawk at this missionary meeting, and said, "I have seen many who professed to know the rules of elocution, and those who carried their principles out in practice, but never before did I see a perfect orator." In the United States William Case introduced the subject at the missionary meetings, and the audiences were thrilled and melted to tears with his narration of the progress of the Gospel among the sons of the forest.

During a visit paid to his friends in the interests of the Canadian Indians, he addressed the Conference Missionary Meeting held at Lansing, N.Y., on August 17th, 1825, in which he is reported to have said many touching and attractive things about the Indians on the Grand River Mission. The people bordering on the reservation were deeply anxious on religious matters, and while the minds of Christian people were engaged in meditating on schemes for sending the Gospel to these Indians, generous donors came forward with help, and God touched the hearts of Crawford, Torry and others, compelling them by the Divine power of love to go forth to toil for the souls of these people.

Blessed results had followed the establishment of the mission, and the ministrations of these faithful men. "The effects of the Gospel have been great and salutary. Many converts might be named; I will mention only a few. A principal chief in the Mohawk nation

BECOMING CIVILIZED.

was a sedate and steady man before, but it was not till he heard the Gospel in its power that he experienced a gracious change. This laid the foundation of that burning zeal for his people, that he exhorts them deeply; and to encourage a school for the youth and children, gave up his own house and retired for the winter to his cabin in the woods. Another had been a great prodigal, having expended in gambling and drunkenness a considerable estate left him by his father. But he had spent all, and was a poor unhappy sinner when he was brought to consider his condition and seek the Saviour. He is now a new man and a happy Christian, and is employed in teaching a school of Indian children among his people.

"The last I shall mention is Peter Jones, of whom mention has been made in the reports and magazines. This youth is a Chippawa (Mississauga) of some education, and of hope and promise to his nation and the Church. Soon after his conversion he commenced a school in his father's house, where he brought the orphans whom he gathered up, and taught them to read, and also taught them the way to heaven. He is now a good exhorter, and speaks his own language and the English fluently. Peter now traverses the forest in search of the wild men of his nation—talks to them of Jesus and the great, good Spirit. By this means a number have been brought to God, among whom is a principal chief who has pitched his tent at the Mission House, and who, with a number of his family, have become members of the Church. This work has now been going on for two years, and such has been the depth and stability of the work, that rarely an instance has occurred of intemperance. The Mississaugas, the most besotted for intoxication, have renounced strong drink altogether. They are now commencing improvements in civilized life, and are very desirous to have their children learn to read the good book. The translation of the Scriptures is going forward in the Mohawk, and the Gospel of St. Luke is now ready for the press. As a further evidence that this work is of God, the converts love one another; they love their enemies; they love their neighbors as themselves. Some centuries ago, the Mohawks, the Cayugas, and other Confederate nations, pitched their tents on the banks of these lakes, where you are now encamped. They made war on the great Chippawa nation, of the northern lakes. Thousands fell, of whose tombs hundreds are now to be seen at the head of Ontario. These wars had created a hatred which ages have not been able to wear away, till lately. The pious Mohawks, who inhabit the richest lands, have said to the Chippawas, 'Come and plant corn on our lands, and send your children to our schools.' And the converted Chippawas, forgetting their former animosity to the Mohawks, are now enjoying the fruits of their fields, and the benefit of the school."

Some of the young men on the Indian reserves, whose hearts the Lord had touched, were accustomed to repair to the woods at sunrise, and there pour out their complaints to God. When the missionaries visited some of these reserves which were under the direction of a school teacher, the people flocked to the place of meeting at the sound of the shell or horn. As regularly as the hour of nine in the morning arrived, one of the Indians blew the horn to call the people to service, and eagerly they responded. Solemnly they knelt in prayer, asking God's blessing upon the service, and in response to a hymn named by the leader or missionary, they sang sweetly in their native Mohawk, Ojibway or Delaware. The missionary sometimes preached through an interpreter, a few sentences being given and then interpreted, but there were occasions on which an Indian of rare intelligence was found able to listen to the entire discourse, and then translate the whole rapidly, without losing a single idea. I have read of instances, which I seriously doubt, of Indians translating a discourse of twenty or thirty minutes' duration, after it had been delivered, without missing a single word or in any way changing the form of a single sentence. From my own experience with interpreters, and my knowledge of the difference in construction between the Indian and English languages, I consider this to be an impossibility, unless a man were gifted with the memory of a Richard Parson. After the missionary's discourse some of the Indians in the audience gave exhortations to the people, and others related their Christian experience, the whole service concluding with prayer by the Indians.

Late in December, 1823, the Rev. James B. Finley, the famous Wyandot missionary, left his home in the Sandusky Mission, in Ohio, and accompanied by three converted Wyandots from the mission, crossed the river Detroit, landing at a camp of the Wyandots on the Canard river, a few miles from the town of Amherstburg, where he intended spending Christmas with the Indians. The Indians preached to their friends, and then the missionary preached for three hours, through an interpreter. Having finished his sermon, he formed those who were desirous of being Christians into a class, of whom twelve signified their intention; and with a leader, this constituted the second Methodist Indian Society in Canada, which was instrumental in doing good to these Indians. The members of the Legislature having heard of the success of the Gospel among the Indians on the Grand River reservation, extended the Common School Act to Indian schools, by which they could participate in Government grants. Torry and Crawford, who had toiled so hard and so effectively among the Mohawks, were at last induced, by home influences and other circumstances, to leave the Indian mission field. Seth Crawford labored for two years among the Mohawks, studying their language, living with them, working as a farmer, teacher and missionary, and very many were led through his devoted example to abandon their heathenism and follow the Master, Christ.

Alvin Torry labored for five years among the Mohawks, and from his lips the Mississaugas and Muncey Indians heard the Gospel. Receiving an appointment in the Genesee Conference, he went there, thus becoming separated from the work which he had begun. The origin of Indian missionary work in Upper Canada must ever have associated with it the names of the pious shoemaker, Edmund Stoney, Alvin Torry, Seth Crawford, William Case and Peter Jones.

These early workers were loved, trusted, and mourned for by the Indians who forsook drunkenness and debauchery through their faithful ministrations. The present condition of the Six Nation Indians as farmers, enjoying excellent social advantages, schools and churches, and surrounded with all the political privileges and discoveries of science and art of the closing years of the nineteenth century, presents a striking contrast to the dawn of the century, when superstition, vice and degradation ruled supreme among the wigwams of the land.

CHAPTER IV.

EVANS' PREDECESSOR.

PETER JONES was a worthy pioneer in the Indian work, striving for the amelioration of the red race, and the glory of his Master. Born at the heights of Burlington Bay, his father, an American of Welsh extraction, and his mother, the daughter of a Mississauga chief, he was trained in all the mysterious lore of the lodges, and spoke with greater fluency the language of the Indians, than that of the other highly favored race. Converted while yet a youth, he began to exercise his talents in teaching school and preaching, and great was the success crowning his efforts in leading men to follow Christ. His soul burned with enthusiasm to tell the depraved dwellers in the wigwams of light and life through the wondrous revelation given to man. He travelled over the province and beyond, organizing camp-meetings, preaching to the Indians in the deep recesses of the forest or in the woods that skirt the lakes. The Indians flocked to hear him in large numbers, and the poor benighted pagan sot forsook his cup and dance, rejoicing in salvation through the atoning sacrifice of Christ.

A request came from an earnest young man who had located among the Muncey Indians, teaching their children, that Peter Jones would pay a visit to these people. This young man, John Carey, had witnessed the degraded condition of these Delaware Indians, and went amongst them to lead them in the path of truth and peace. Many years before this time the ancestors of this people had listened to the preaching of David Brainerd, and when persecuted they had sought a refuge in Canada. Jones and his companions made two visits to the Indian camps, and were gratified at seeing success.

In 1825, the first report of the Methodist Missionary Society was issued, which dealt with the work and its needs. Missionary labor was confined to the needy white settlers and the Indian tribes. Deep interest had been taken in the Six Nations and Ojibway Indians, and the report deals principally with the native religious ideas and customs, and the origin, progress and successes of the missions.

Many souls had been won for the Master, and the power of the new ideas had been witnessed in the birth of a true and ennobling civilization. Christianity, preceding civilization, had produced it. And so soon as the impulse of a new affection had been felt, the people asked for schools and teachers that their children might be educated, and sternly opposed vice, drunkenness, and superstition in all its forms.

These were the ever-recurring effects of Christianity among the Indians on the reservations, and stronger proofs than these were not needed to convince the red men of the genuineness and blessedness of the Christian religion. Better clothing and consequent self-respect, neater and more comfortable buildings, kindlier treatment of the young and the women in the camps, and the absence of war between the tribes were some of the fruits of the seed sown.

Dr. A. Hill, an educated Mohawk chief, translated the four Gospels into the Mohawk tongue, and an intelligent young lady, daughter of one of the chiefs, the Acts of the Apostles.

In February, 1826, William Case and Peter Jones went on a missionary tour to the Bay of Quinte Indians, and held a meeting in Belleville attended by white people and Indians. The morning service was well attended, and in the evening Jones discoursed to a large concourse of Indians on "The Two Ways." Two Indians unable to get inside the church in the morning sat outside, but found in the evening a place with the worshippers. The arrow of conviction pierced their hearts, but peace came not to their minds until in May following they heard again the truth, and were raised from depths of degradation to rejoice in purity and dignity of character and life.

Shawundais, better known amongst the white

people as John Sunday, after having learned to read and write, narrated the circumstance described, when he and Moses listened intensely to the discourse of Peter Jones. John Sunday became a zealous missionary to his own people, and by his quaint methods of

AN OLD-TIMER.

speech and forcible manner of expressing himself, he was able to lead many to the Saviour's side. Dark and benighted child of the woods, nursed in the lap of superstition, haunted by the spirits of the rapids, rocks and trees, debauched by immoral white men, or taunted by his own people, he found at last life, and in that life there came blessed toil which brought salvation for his body and intellect.

Sunday and Jones together toiled and rejoiced in the fruit of their labors.

A great camp-meeting was held at Adolphustown, where nearly one hundred Indians professed conversion.

Sunday and several other Indian exhorters were there, telling in accents of new-found love the story of the Calvary Cross. It was a wonderful story and a strange meeting. The Indians knew only one tune and a single hymn, but that one the song of missionary lands.

> "Oh for a thousand tongues to sing
> My great Redeemer's praise."

Over and over again they sang it, with increased fervor and hope, until souls were ushered into the kingdom by the power of the Gospel in song.

The Conference of 1826 was held on the Cobourg Circuit, presided over by Bishop George, and blessed with the presence of Dr. Bangs. The Indians flocked to the Conference to hear greater things concerning God's love to man; but anxious to receive all the blessings possible for them to enjoy, they held a camp-meeting at Cramahe a few days before the opening of the Conference. Ministers and laymen were there, and as the songs of Zion ascended to heaven, sung in the English and Ojibway languages, the power of God fell upon the hearts of the people, and twenty of the pagan Indians professed to have received the pardon of sin. During the Conference the Indians pitched their camp in the vicinity of the church where the ministers were assembled, anxious to learn more of God's will. The report of God's doings among the red men spread among the Indian camps scattered throughout the forests, and some of them came to see and hear. A band of Indians from Rice Lake, accompanied by their chief was present, and when Dr. Bangs addressed the Indians in the camp, they all listened with intense earnestness. The Doctor asked the chief, through an interpreter, why he had come to the meeting, and with the gravity and dignity of an Indian chief, he replied, "I heard, while in the forest, of the great work going on among my people; and I came down to see and hear and examine for myself." "Are you convinced of the evil of your former habits?" "Yes." "How did you feel when convinced of your sinfulness?" Putting his hand to his heart, he said, "I felt very sick here, I now feel well—happy."

This was the beginning of the work among the Rice Lake Indians, and the evidences of the genuineness of the change that had taken place was seen in the rejection of intoxicating drinks, and the new life of sobriety, cleanliness and joy that had come to the camp.

The influence of the Gospel upon the Indians was remarkable, and the white people were not slow to notice this, whilst some of them were desirous of giving encouragement to the red men to continue in the way of truth.

At a missionary meeting held at Demorestville, attended by the Indians, a Mississauga youth, named Jacob Peter, eighteen years of age, was requested to address the white people present in the English language, which he did in a forcible manner, as follows: "You white people have the Gospel great many years. You have the Bible, too; suppose you read it sometimes—but you very wicked. Suppose some very good people; you get drunk; you tell lies; you break the Sabbath." Pointing to the Indians present, he continued, "But these Indians, they hear the Word only a little while; they can't read the Bible; but they become good right away. They no more get drunk, no more tell lies, they keep the Sabbath day. To us Indians, seems very strange that you have missionary so many years, and you so many *rogues yet.* The Indians have missionary only little while, and we all turn Christian."

Jones, Sunday and Case were in labors abundant

among the red men, and not contented with visiting the Indians, they attended missionary meetings, telling the people of the wonderful works of grace.

At the ninth anniversary of the Methodist Episcopal Missionary Society, held in New York, Case and Sunday were present, and addressed the large congregation. Peter Jacobs, an Indian youth, was present, and after reading the parable of the lost sheep, in English and Ojibway, with such pathos as visibly affected the people, he gave an account of his conversion. Dr. Bangs spoke to Sunday, having Peter Jacobs as interpreter, and then in the name of the congregation gave him the right hand of Christian fellowship, expressing the hope that they would all meet in heaven.

When Sunday heard the words of the Christian minister, as interpreted by Jacobs, the tears coursed down his cheeks, and he sobbed aloud, many in the audience weeping with him, as he said in response to their prayers, "Amen! Amen!" When Case and Sunday related to the Indians on the reserves what they had seen and heard, they were filled with astonishment. Sunday was somewhat doubtful as to the religion of some of the people, and felt deeply anxious for their souls' welfare. He said to the Indians in the course of his address, "When I look on their fine houses and other riches and great conveniences, I have feared that the hearts of Christians here are not prepared to leave it. But when I hear them pray, and see their concern for the poor, the children and the Indians, I must think them good Christians, and hope to meet them in heaven." The work spread among the Indians at Lake Simcoe, some of the Mohawks at Tyendinaga accepted the Gospel and were blessed, and many triumphant deaths were witnessed in the wigwams.

Polly Ryckman, of the Grand River Mission, died with a smile upon her countenance saying, "I feel that Jesus is round about my bed all the time, and I know the Great Spirit will receive me in to heaven. I am not afraid to die. Oh! how merciful, how glorious is the Great Spirit! My heart is full of joy. Oh! that all my brothers and sisters might be faithful in serving Kezha Munedoo!" The wife of Peter Jacobs died trusting in God, and John Cameron—Wageezhegomes, the possessor of day—passed to the land beyond the river, rejoicing in Christ. He had been a wayward youth, cared for by an Indian trader and living a wild, reckless life until his conversion, when he became a useful man among his people, utilizing his knowledge of the English language for their benefit. Four years only he lived after giving his heart to God, but they were years of usefulness. During his last sickness he said, "I thank the Lord that I have lived to see all my people serve the Great Spirit. For many years past I have again and again wished the good white Christian might come and plant the Christian religion among us, and teach us the right way we should go. But no one cared for our souls, until the Lord Himself raised up one of our own people to tell us what we must do to be saved: and now I can depart in peace, and go to our Great Father in heaven."

In the early years of Indian mission work the best men were chosen as missionaries, amongst whom we need only mention Egerton Ryerson, afterward city minister, college president and Superintendent of Education for Upper Canada, whose monument stands in front of the Normal School, Toronto, but whose enduring memorial is the educational system of Ontario. The native laborers went from camp to camp, telling the story of redeeming love. Far and wide the news spread of the advent of the Man of Nazareth, and on bended knee the painted warrior knelt, owning allegiance to the Christ. Portions of the Scriptures were translated into the Mohawk and Ojibway languages, and several hymns were arranged to be sung by the Indians in public worship and at home.

The camps no longer resounded with the war-whoop or savage yell of the debauched Indian, but from the wigwams the songs of Christian worship arose on the evening air, significant token of peace, purity and divine love.

NORTHERN RIVER.

CHAPTER V.

RICE LAKE.

TWELVE miles north of Cobourg lies an inland lake, whose waters are received from the northern lakes through the Otonabee river, and are then emptied by the rapid Trent into the Bay of Quinte. Large quantities of wild rice grow in the lake, furnishing food for wild fowl and Indians, and from the existence of this grain, the sheet of water is called Rice Lake. In the year eighteen hundred and twenty-six, a band of Ojibway Indians, under Chief Patosh, lived in the woods skirting the lake, and these people were known as the Rice Lake Indians. There were other bands related to these dwelling at lakes Mud and Scugog, and known respectively as the Mud Lake and Lake Scugog Indians. Members of these bands visited Peterborough and Port Hope to barter their furs with the Indian traders, who were sometimes men of good education but immoral and greedy of gain. Visits made to these trading posts resulted in debauchery, poverty and crime. Liquor was sold to the Indians, and the furs were then bought at a reduced price. When the missionaries began their work among the red men there arose an antagonism between them and the traders, as no longer were the drunken natives cheated; but when sobriety, peace and industry dwelt in the camps, the full value for the furs was demanded, and articles of usefulness sought in exchange.

When the Conference was held near Hull's Corners, about three miles north of Cobourg, an invitation had been sent to the pagan Indians of Rice Lake to attend the Cramahe camp-meeting and the religious services of the Conference. Chief Catosh and a large number of his Indians were present, most of them being led to Christ during the meeting. The Chief, in broken English, expressed his joy by saying. "Oh! Ho! Me never think meeting feel so good!" The Mud Lake and Lake Scugog Indians were brought to God through the instrumentality of Peter Jones and his fellow-workers. The Rice Lake Indians were visited occasionally by Peter Jones, and so great was the Christian joy of the people, that they shouted, wept and prayed. The traders acknowledged that they were sober, honest, cleanly and industrious as the result of the Gospel. They commenced farming under the guidance of the missionary, and built a brush church in which to hold public worship. The days were spent in farming, and the evening in worshipping God in the brush church. Before leaving in the autumn for their hunting expedition, they requested the missionary to organize a school, and they left behind them the women and children, so that they might have the benefits of education. A school-house was erected in the winter of 1827, and H. Biggar engaged as teacher. On the south shore of the lake stood the school and church, where sixty children were taught by the teacher and boarded by their parents. When the Indians returned from the winter hunt, meetings were held which were seasons of joy, and eighty-five of the natives partook of the sacrament of the Lord's Supper, while ninety-six church members were returned at the Conference of 1828.

The Rice Lake school was the eighth Indian school in operation under the Methodist Missionary Society, and so deeply attached were the Indian women to their children and so anxious for education to be given them, that they went to the villages every few days to sell baskets and other articles of their own manufacture, that they might be able to procure food. Hindrances arose toward the final victory of the Gospel among the people, by visits from members of other tribes who came to "make medicine," gamble and indulge in native feasts and sacrifices, and from the vanity and childish spirit manifested by some of the people who spent their earnings in gaudy dresses, trinkets and unnecessary luxuries.

The school was taught by Miss Ashe, and then by

Miss Barnes, who came from the United States to engage in missionary work, and finally became the second wife of the Rev. William Case.

By the help of the native class leaders and local preachers, among whom were Peter Rice Lake, and Allan and J. Crow, the work of grace was efficiently carried on among the band.

In the autumn of 1828, James Evans was engaged. to teach the Indian school at Rice Lake. Two years previously he and his devoted wife had experienced the favor of God at the Augusta camp-meeting, and, still rejoicing in divine love, and blessed with an excellent education, the keen eye of William Case saw the stuff the man was made of, and recognized the saintliness of the woman. As a teacher he displayed those qualities of mind and heart which fitted him in an eminent degree for the position of a missionary to the red men. He began the study of the Ojibway language, and rapidly gained a knowledge of its principles and grammatical construction, which enabled him in a short time to address the Indians in their own tongue. He grappled so successfully with the intricacies of the language, that he began to translate portions of the Scriptures and hymns for the use of the tribes speaking the Ojibway form of speech. He was ever cheerful in the most trying circumstances, and was able to become master of every difficulty. A friend visiting the mission found the teacher and his family possessed of a small quantity of flour, the only kind of food in the house. Mixing it with some fish spawn, they made pancakes of it, and partook heartily of the best they had. Poverty and hardship were accepted complacently as part of the missionary's lot. Daunted not by the greatest obstacles, victory was sure to follow. The man was so thoroughly imbued with the spirit of his Master, aroused by a holy enthusiasm for souls, determined to succeed and able to engage in any kind of manual labor, that everything he touched seemed to prosper.

William Case visited the United States in the interests of his Indian missions, and was successful in obtaining funds to print there translations of portions of the New Testament in Mohawk and Ojibway, made by Peter Jones; and during this period, James Evans was busily employed in his school, helping the Indians in manual labor, and studying the language. For one year and a half he toiled hard among the members of the Rice Lake band, and assisted the Rev. D. McMillan, who was minister of the Cavan and Rice Lake Mission.

At the Conference of 1830, which began its sessions in Kingston on August 17th, James Evans was received on probation for the ministry. This Conference adjourned on the 24th to meet at Belleville, as the General Conference was to meet there, but the stations were read at Kingston. This Conference is worthy of remembrance, for the chief subject of its deliberations was the instituting of a seminary of learning for the Methodists and the general public of the Province, which resulted finally in the establishment of Upper Canada Academy, known latterly as Victoria University. Our probationer had given him as his work the Rice Lake and Mud Lake bands of Indians, which he managed efficiently, but towards the end of the year he had to superintend the Cavan Circuit, with its seventeen appointments, and was thus heavily burdened with work. Peter Jones was appointed by the Conference General Missionary to the Indian tribes, and in this capacity he visited the Rice Lake Mission, when he and the missionary there went on a visit to the Mud Lake Indians, noting progress in farming, education and piety.

William Case manifested great interest in the work of translating the Scriptures, in which he was heartily supported by Jones and Evans. Jones, Evans and Thomas Hurlburt were the men who laid the foundation of Indian linguistic study, and great success followed their first attempt at translating God's truth. James Evans translated eighteen chapters of Genesis and twenty Psalms, besides preparing a vocabulary of the Ojibway language, which were given to Peter Jones for correction, and to serve as a guide for other translations. The missionaries believed that by help of these translations much good would be done toward equipping the missionary workers, besides spreading the truth among the Indians. William Case, in writing to Peter Jones, who was in England, becomes enthusiastic over the work of the Indian missionaries: "Our field of labor is very extensive, extending from Lower Canada to Lake Huron and Mackinaw, an extent of not less than eight hundred miles, embracing ten bodies or tribes of Indians, including sixteen schools, four hundred and twenty children, employing eight white and nine native missionaries. All praise to the Great Shepherd! Five of these bodies—Grape Island, Rice Lake, Simcoe, Sah-geeng, River Credit—have all embraced Christianity, have all become a praying people. The work is now going on for the conversion of four of the other bodies out of the five, namely, Bay of Quinte, Grand River, Munceytown, and Mackinaw. All of the missions, as far as we hear, are progressing. I should also have mentioned that six persons are engaged in the translation of the Scriptures into the Iroquois and Chippawa language. When those Scriptures are translated and printed, and when the four hundred Indian children shall be reading to their parents and friends, and when ten and even twenty native missionaries shall be travelling from tribe to tribe through the forests, enforcing the Divine Word among thirty thousand wandering natives of our wilderness, and when God shall add His blessing for the conversion of these, as He has done in the conversion already of eighteen hundred, what may we not expect but the fulfilment of prophecy, "The wilderness and the solitary place shall be made glad for them, and the desert shall rejoice and blossom as the rose?"*

Part of another letter to Peter Jones, on the same important subject of translations, reveals Mr. Case's views on this special department of Indian missionary work: "There is no part of the missionary work to which your attention can now be directed more important than that of translating the Scriptures for the use of our Indian brethren, hundreds of whom can now read, and are desirous of learning more perfectly the way of the Lord; and it is a matter of gratification that you are at length relieved from the labors and journeyings which have, in a degree, interrupted this important work. The Gospels of Matthew and John are now being distributed to the Indians, and may be studied while other important portions are preparing for their use. I am of opinion that the other two Gospels and the Epistles should be deferred for a while, and that we should labor to complete the book of Genesis, which has for some time been under

* "Case and his Contemporaries."

consideration. The reasons which influence this opinion, are: 1. That the two Gospels, now in the hands of the Indians, are enough for the present, till they shall have read and studied them, when they will be better prepared to commence the reading of other portions of the New Testament. 2. That Dr. James, of Ste. Marie, we understand, has gone through the whole New Testament in the Chippawa, and that the work is being published. Till we know the merits of that work we had better defer further translations of the New Testament. It may answer every purpose without further expense, at least for the present. 3. The knowledge of the great works of creation, and first transactions of man, which are found in Genesis, are scarcely less valuable to remove pagan superstitions and give a right direction to the faith of the Indian converts. Wishing to put into the hands of the Indians the nine first chapters of the book of Genesis, if one thousand copies be printed, a few hundred of which —say, two hundred and fifty—might be soon done up for the use of the schools, etc., and the remainder remain till the rest shall be printed, and then all done up together. It will be printed on opposite pages with the English."

The Gospel spread rapidly among the tribes, so that the red men of the forest sat at the feet of Jesus, clothed and in their right mind. There were many promising young men led to Christ in the Indian camp who became deeply concerned for their companions and friends.

On the Grape Island Mission a young people's prayer-meeting was held regularly every Monday.

THE RAPIDS.

At one of these meetings, John Kennedy—Shippegah—aged fourteen years, prayed fervently for his comrades: "O Kezhe Mûnedo! Sha-wa nim ope no gee uck a-ah-chick Mah-quayah-quah a-ah-ze-kook, muz-ee-nee-ah-gun-nun kia meenzheke-he-noo-mah-te-win. Che-ah-kin-moo-wadt, muz-ee-ah-gun-nun." "O great good Spirit, bless the children in the woods who have no books, and give them schools that they may learn to read!"

Thus not only the adult population, but the children, heard with joy the words of life. Had many of these bright lads been sent to college, we should have had teachers and native missionaries well qualified for the work, and in sufficient numbers to supply all the demands of their tribes.

The enterprising and catholic-spirited Evans rejoiced in such manifestations of good, and ever eager for greater success, employed every legitimate agency for leading men and women to God. Burning with zeal for the souls of men, he studied the language, taught the children, toiled in the fields with the men, translated, preached, prayed and lived near to God.

CHAPTER VI.

THE CREDIT.

THE first Methodist Indian mission in Canada was begun amongst the Mohawks at Grand River in 1822. Peter Jones was converted at the Ancaster camp-meeting in 1823, and the Mississauga Indians, living around Belleville, received the Gospel in 1826. The most successful of all the Indian missions of this early period was the Credit Mission, arising from the constant supervision of William Case, and the able men who assisted him. This was the home of Peter Jones, who travelled extensively among the tribes scattered throughout the Province, preaching to them and directing them in all affairs relating to their political, social and agricultural life. His translations were carried on at home, where he received the assistance of Indians. Egerton Ryerson was for a time missionary at the Credit, sent there through the influence of William Case, who believed that he would be instrumental in preparing a grammar and dictionary of the Ojibway language, and in translating the Scriptures, thus removing serious difficulties out of the way of others. Young Ryerson toiled with the Indians in the field, preached and prayed, and built a church with funds which he raised himself. His brother George was missionary at the Credit in after years, and Edwy Ryerson followed as teacher of the Indian school. James Evans spent one year among the Indians at the Credit. The Government had advised the Mississaugas to leave the Grand River and repair to the Credit, promising to build a village for the Indians at that place. The people went there, spending the summer at the Credit hunting and fishing, and the winter at Grand River. A brush chapel was erected by the Indians, and school began with forty children. The Government erected twenty hewed log houses, and Egerton Ryerson toiled earnestly among them. In 1825, the Parliament being assembled at Toronto (York), about twenty of the school children were taken to the embryo city, and appeared in public in the Methodist church. The speaker of the assembly occupied the chair, and after the children had sung some hymns in English and Indian, recited the Ten Commandments, read portions of the Scriptures, and exhibited specimens of writing and sewing, several of the members of Parliament gave addresses of approval. The following day they went on invitation of Lady Maitland to Government House, and were examined before the Governor, who was well pleased with the improvement made in their studies, and gave presents to the children.

A few days afterward Governor Maitland and party paid a visit to the Credit, visiting the homes of the Indians, and the schools, and expressed himself as delighted with the signs of progress, industry and peace. James Evans was sent by the Conference of 1831 as missionary to the Credit. Here were displayed his talents in translating portions of the Scriptures and hymns; and with ever-increasing enthusiasm he continued his studies in the construction of the language of the people among whom he labored. He toiled with the people in the fields, superintending their farms, directed the educational work of the mission, went in and out of the homes of the natives, telling them in their own tongue the wonderful things of God. Deeply sympathetic, he sought to comfort the lonely mourner, and lead gently, with sweet, persuasive words, to the cross of Christ. Energetic and enterprising as he was, he could not rest contented while he witnessed the white population, living in the vicinity of the Indian reservation, without a knowledge of Christ. The time that he could spare from the Indian work was given to the white settlers, and he enjoyed the satisfaction of seeing some brought into the way of life. His translations increased, and were more accurate. Souls were saved, and the people were happy and prosperous. At the Conference of 1832, he was sent to take charge of the Ancaster

Mission, which included the embryo city of Hamilton, and there he displayed superior abilities as a preacher, administrator and pastor. His colleague was Edwy M. Ryerson, and their united labors were blessed with a gracious outpouring of God's Spirit, insomuch that several hundred persons were converted to God. Amongst these were Edward and Lydia Jackson, so prominent afterwards in Canadian Methodist history, and especially remembered in the city of Hamilton, and in connection with Victoria University, Cobourg. Faithful to the souls he had won for Christ, James Evans confronted fearlessly any form of doctrine that would injure what he had done. Boldly and successfully he opposed Elijah Warren, who had imbibed the principles of Universalism, and was teaching them to the people.

In the year following, the Conference stationed this intrepid servant of God at St. Catharines, with John Baxter as his colleague, and the work done there sufficiently attested the fact that when able men were needed for important positions they could find one in the devoted and versatile preacher of St. Catharines. He stood well with his ministerial brethren, because of his sterling worth, for he was oftentimes compelled, in the stirring times in which he lived, to oppose his best friends. Friendship was nothing to principle; and though he dearly loved his friends, he loved the truth more. Those were stirring times for the Methodist Church, and in all her concerns he was ever in the front to defend her interests when they were on the side of truth.

At the Conference of 1833, before being sent to St. Catharines, he was ordained, and from that moment,

DOG-TRAIN SQUABBLE.

more fully than ever, did he enter into the work to which he had devoted his life.

This was to be his last year in the white work, for God and man had designated him for pioneer work among the aborigines of Canada; and the events that followed justified the men in studying God's providence and becoming submissive thereto.

CHAPTER VII.

ST. CLAIR.

ON the present site of Sarnia, and at several points along the River St. Clair, were located bands of Ojibway Indians who had not accepted the Gospel of Christ. The Lieutenant-Governor had instituted measures for assisting these people, but owing to their nomadic habits, the adjacent residence of white men, whose influence was for evil, and the degraded lives which they had spent, they failed to elevate them. The Colonial Government then called upon the Wesleyan Missionary authorities of England to undertake missionary work amongst them, and the parent body felt in duty bound to extend its operations to the red men of Canada. In accordance with this determimation, and the invitation of the Canadian Government, the work was inaugurated by sending the Rev. Thomas Turner to begin his labors among the St. Clair Indians. He entered heartily upon his field in 1832, and encountered customs and beliefs, superstitions and errors, antagonistic to his work, and not understood by the white race. The missionary found a kind of life that was strange, full of hardship, and distasteful. Unacquainted with Indian life and the severe toils of the early settlers, surrounded by influences opposed to the truth, peace and purity of the Christian religion, and with few to give him encouragement in his arduous work, he found the difficulties so numerous and heavy that there came not the success he desired and prayed for. This was to be expected from the debauched condition of the Indians, and the immoral example set before them by the Indian traders. In 1834 James Evans was sent to prosecute his missionary work on the field where Mr. Turner had failed, and possessed of those peculiar traits of character which revealed the man's ability to adapt himself to all kinds of men and every variety of life, great things were looked for on his new mission. The friends of missions had not long to wait, as he entered upon his work with his accustomed energy. Preaching, translating, teaching school, building houses, and directing young and old in all affairs temporal and spiritual. The Indians caught the enthusiasm of the devoted missionary, and were ready to follow where he led. They forsook the haunts of the white men and resorted to nobler ways of living, encouraged by the sympathies of their leader and the evidences of prosperity in the homes of their fellows The news of the adjacent bands and tribes receiving the Gospel reached their ears, and proved an incentive to industry, purity and faithfulness in the good cause. David Sawyer, an Indian teacher and interpreter, toiling amongst the Indians at Muncey Town, relates a circumstance that must have produced beneficial effects upon the other Indians. He says: "Our principal labours are in Upper and Lower Muncey. We have had three deaths of late. Two were remarkable, their contrast was so great. The persons were Highflyer and Necaunaby. The former, being tempted by the rum-seller, drank to that degree that the alcoholic principle extinguished the vital spark. The scene was appalling beyond the power of language to describe. I am told that his seducer is a believer that all will be saved. Does he believe that he sent this man's soul to heaven in the midst of his days? The latter is among some of the first ripe fruits of the humble missionary's labors. His complaint was consumption, to which they are alarmingly subject. We visited him during the days of his rapid decline. It was truly affecting to see him lift his emaciated hands towards heaven, and pour out his soul to his Heavenly Father in strains of eloquence sufficient to convince us, at least, that the Spirit helped his infirmities. His prayers rose on the wings of faith; the precious name of Jesus faltered on his tongue to the last, while the big tears rolled down his face; and even when his eyes had ceased to weep, a little before he died, he told the people who were present, "I am very poor; yes, I am very sick; but I shall be very rich in heaven, when I get home. I am very happy." He would sometimes say, "O Jesus! O Jesus!" Just a short time before he died, he gave a little exhortation to those present. "Now my brothers and sisters," he said, "I am going to leave you very soon. The angels told me that I must come in about an hour; I see the angels around me waiting in that house." And he would tell his brethren, "The angels are talking to me." Being asked what the angels said, he replied, "Don't you hear? They say to me that I shall see my child in Ishpeming" (heaven). Again he said, "Give me your hands. I shake hands with you all, my brothers and sisters, for I am going to leave you soon; you must be faithful." He also told them, "Be silent, for I am waiting my departure." Having said this, he gently fell asleep in Jesus' arms, without a sigh or a groan, to wake again at the last trump; "for the trumpet shall sound, and the dead shall be raised." Then Highflyer and the rum-seller must meet, as well as the missionary and Necaunaby."

Success in the conversion of the red men followed the labors of James Evans among the St. Clair Indians. The Rev. Dr. Evans, now residing in London, Ontario, referring to his brother's success on the St. Clair Mission at this period, says: "A sweeping tide of converting power changed the entire character of the tribe, and greatly stimulated him to a critical study of the language, and to the translation of portions of the Holy Scriptures, and a publication of the translation of many of the Methodist hymns. To this day his name is as ointment poured forth in the memories of the few aged persons still remaining, who, through his instrumentality, were rescued from the chains and bondage of paganism, and translated into the kingdom of His dear Son."

By pen and voice the faithful toiler sought to enlist the sympathies of Christian people on behalf of his work among the Indians, and succeeded in a great measure in arousing a deep interest in the cause of the red man.

OOZHUSHKAH.

The following sketch of an Ojibway Indian named Oozhushkah, and the two subsequent letters written by James Evans, will be read with pleasure by all students of missions and friends of the red man, and especially by all who wish to learn more of the faithful apostle who toiled at Sarnia, striving to direct to God and truth :

"Oozhushkah, a native Indian of the Chippewa tribe now resides at Mackinaw. He was once one of the lowest and most abandoned of that profligate class of Indians, who have measurably forsaken their native wilds, and linger about the settlements of the whites.

His stature is small, his frame worn down with age and debilitated by former dissipation presents a strange ghastliness of appearance, which strikes the beholder with involuntary awe, and, to a superstitious mind, almost excites the belief that Oozhushkah is a deserter from the land of departed spirits. But however fearful and suspicious the character of Oozhushkah may have once been, those acquainted with his present character do not now fear him ; for his spirit, formerly wild and untamable, is at present the home of gentleness and meekness; once dark and intriguing, is now honest and guileless. It is his former character that has imprinted upon him his fearful physiognomy, for the spirit of Christianity has touched his heart and subdued his native ferocity; and instead of joining his companions in the brutal and destroying revels of drunkenness, his chief delight is in offering up his hearty orisons to the God of his salvation.

"It is well known to those familiar with Indian history that they have among them a certain class of persons called prophets, or conjurors, who profess to foretell future events by a direct conference with the Great Spirit. These are supposed to possess a decided superiority over other men, having a guardian deity acquainted at all times with their danger, ready and able to communicate to them a knowledge of it, and to deliver them from it. In consequence of this prevalent opinion, those who have been at any time most celebrated among the Indians, and who have gained a proud pre-eminence over their people, either in the character of statesmen or warriors, have always assumed the reputation of prophets; and even at this day the young men of the northern tribes cannot be induced to follow any leader in war, unless he is supposed to have more or less communication with the Great Spirit. Some of these professed prophets are the most abandoned of the Indians, and, while they are hated for their vices, are viewed with fear and dread for the unconquerable power they are supposed to possess. Such was once Oozhushkah. His name stood unrivalled as a prophet, and he was considered invincible as a warrior. If he treated the proudest of the unbending savages with indignity and disdain, they feared to retaliate; for death in strange and unheard-of shapes, sometimes by slow, and sometimes by rapid poison, seized the enemies of Oozhushkah. His eye seemed never to slumber, and every art to ensnare or surprise him failed. In short, he appeared as secure as he was terrible. A strange mysteriousness enveloped him; and tradition says, that though he was one of the smallest and most meagre of the Indians, he was once weighed by a trader, and to the astonishment of of all, weighed upwards of three hundred pounds. Oozhushkah had, for a number of the last years, hung about the trading house of Mackinaw, and was well known as one of the most abandoned and drunken of his race. The missionaries stationed at that post had often faithfully tried to instruct him in the knowledge of that God who made, preserved and redeemed him; but Oozhushkah had always responded to their instructions with the most supercilious contempt, and their lessons were apparently "pearls cast before swine." But they were not lost. They were securely lodged in the retentive memory of Oozhushkah. He narrated them to his wife, who was as drunken as himself; but when sober these lessons formed a fruitful theme of conversation. Again and again they were repeated at evening in his tent, and opposed with all the virulence which the natural heart is wont to raise up against truth intended to correct, control, and reform it. But it appears Heaven did not leave them to their desperation.

"In the winter, as usual, Oozhushkah chose his hunting ground some forty or fifty miles from Mackinaw; here, with no human companion but his aged squaw, he pitched his lonely tent, deep in the recesses of the forest. Here, the inebriating draught, the drunken Indian's god, was beyond their reach, they had time for reflection and converse. They had not long occupied their lonely quarters when Mekagase, the squaw, was taken violently ill.

"Oozhushkah's conjuring songs and Indian medicines could not cure her. From day to day she only grew worse. Neither she nor Oozhushkah expected her recovery; but during this illness Mekagase retained her senses. The truth of heaven which she had heard dwelt upon her mind—her own understanding told her she was a wretch, a sinner; that she had all her lifetime persisted in doing knowingly and wilfully wrong. Death stared her in the face, and, like other wicked mortals, she was afraid to die. Her conscience, corroborating what she had learned from the missionaries, convinced her that she was unprepared for death, and that, as a consequence of her wickedness here, she might expect misery hereafter. She was afraid to meet the Great Spirit against whose laws she had offended. Mekagase, trembling on the threshold of eternity saw no remedy; she humbled herself, prayed to the Great Spirit in compassion to forgive her, to blot out her sins and receive her departing spirit. Suddenly, the fears of Mekagase were taken away, joy filled her heart, and she felt indescribably more happy than when in youth she had joined the Indian dance around the evening fires of her tribe. In short, if her own simple description of her feelings may be relied on, she experienced what the apostle designates "joy unspeakable and full of glory." From that hour Mekagase's disease abated and her recovery commenced. She felt that she was a new creature, and, unlike too many enlightened Christians, she did not reason herself out of the faith, but taking the simple testimony of the Spirit bearing witness with her own, spoke of her hopes and her joys to Oozhushkah, with ecstasy and confidence; she warned him of his folly, his wickedness and his danger with so strong convincing testimony, that the heart of Oozhushkah was moved. He prayed to the Great Spirit, and the work of grace was deepened. The radiance of divine truth beamed on his benighted understanding and melted his hardened heart, and in ten days from his wife's singular conversion, Oozhuskah could heartily join with her in offering their morning and evening orisons to the Great Spirit in praise of redeeming grace.

"When the hunting season was over, they returned

THUNDER CAPE.

to Mackinaw, where they lost no time in making known to their Christian acquaintances the change wrought in their feelings; and from that day to this, they have tested both the verity of their conversion, and the salutary influence of gospel truth, by 'well-ordered lives and godly conversation.' They have abandoned the intoxicating liquor, live peaceably with each other, and the once malignant Oozhushkah is now harmless as a lamb; and dark, mysterious and suspicious as his character was formerly, no one acquainted with him at present doubts, or can doubt, of his conversion."

AN INDIAN CAMP-MEETING.

"The spot selected by the Indian chiefs and myself for the purpose was on the bank of the St. Clair River, having a gentle declination toward the water, and admirably adapted by nature's God to seat a congregation in such a manner as to give to all the best possible opportunity of seeing and hearing in the open air. The Indians were much elated in prospect of this meeting; some of whom, having first tasted the joys of salvation at a similar one at Muncey Town, and being instructed from Holy Writ that God is everywhere present, confided in Him for His promised presence on the St. Clair, while several who had never enjoyed such a privilege were anxious to taste those blessings of which their converted friends often spoke with ecstacy. All readily and perseveringly engaged in clearing the ground, which we found in a state of nature, strewed with the trunks of old trees which had once reared their stately heads and bid defiance for ages to the howling tempest, but which had at length fallen before the unsparing scythe of time. These were cut in pieces and drawn off the ground. The underbrush or small trees were also cut down and formed into a sort of hedge or fence, while the large trees were left in all their majestic grandeur, towering over our heads, forcibly reminding us, while sheltered by their luxuriant foliage, of the promise of Him whom we were met to adore, 'The sun shall not smite thee by day, nor the moon by night.'

"The pulpit or preacher's stand was erected near the centre of the ground. This was formed by driving large poles of about twelve or fifteen feet in length into the ground, and laying upon them other poles of sufficient strength to support the floor and roof. The preacher's stand was about twelve feet square, with a partition running through the centre; the front occupied by day as a pulpit, where the speaker declared the Word of Life, while the other preachers sat behind him on a seat prepared for this purpose. The rear of the stand was occupied by night as a bedroom. The seats for the accommodation of the congregation were constructed by splitting large trees into halves or quarters, according to their size, and placing these pieces in front of the pulpit, raised to a convenient height by laying logs beneath them. Of these we prepared sufficient to seat about one thousand persons, which, although rough in appearance, answered the desired purpose, and were occupied with much profit during the exercises of the meeting. A tent for the accommodation of the preachers, and such strangers as might attend who could not bring tents for themselves, was prepared of boards; and we were kindly furnished by the commanding officer at Fort Gratiot, on the American side of the river, with a canvas tent and fly, which proved an excellent shelter, and accommodated the females, who occupied it as a sleeping room. The Indians' tents were made of forked poles driven into the ground, and others laid across, supporting a roof formed of bark, which had been previously peeled off the bass-wood and black ash trees, in sheets of about eight feet in length, and four or five in breadth. Small stakes were driven around and interwoven with small branches, the leaves of which formed an excellent wall, and excluded all observation from without. Some of these tents were twenty feet in length, and ten or twelve in breadth; bark was laid on the ground as a floor. In front of each tent two forked poles were driven into the ground and a pole laid across, to which hooks, made of small branches, were suspended, on which kettles were hung for the purpose of preparing the victuals, as all the provisions were cooked on the ground in the intervals of the religious exercises.

"The day of commencement having arrived, we assembled on the ground, and the services of the meeting were opened with a lively and profitable prayer-meeting in the tent belonging to the head chief, Wawanosh. The grace of supplication was poured out upon our brethren, and many ardent petitions ascended the Hill of Zion for a profitable meeting. Nor were they in vain. The Lord graciously visited us with salvation, and the place became glorious by reason of His presence. Brother Brockway (from the Ohio Conference) and myself preached on Thursday, and several times we engaged in prayer-meetings. On Friday we had preaching twice; and just at the close of the second sermon our brethren the President of the Conference and the General Superintendent of Missions, together with two of the members of our Society from Montreal, cheered us by entering the encampment, and spent with us the remainder of the season of worship in the grove.

"Many of the Christian Indians from the Muncey village on the River Thames, and some from the Credit Mission, this day joined us, and several pagans also were within the encampment. The preaching was pointed and spiritual, and attended by the divine unction. The Gospel plan of salvation was clearly set forth before these sons of the forest in all its enchanting beauty, and the two-edged sword of the Lord Jehovah appeared to cut its way to many a heart; the wounded soul fled to the prayer-meeting after each sermon, and there, with strong cries and tears, sought (and not in vain) for the "balm of Gilead." The good Physician was at hand, and poured in the oil and the wine—healing and cheering; and the sound of joy and gladness resounded throughout the leafy temple.

"On Sunday evening, as a pagan family were sailing down the river in their canoe, their attention was drawn to the place of worship by hearing the voices of the Indians and seeing the ground lighted by the fires which were kindled on stages covered with earth, erected for the purpose. They supposed that it was some Indian pagan feast, and were desirous to "join the fun," as they expressed themselves, expecting that. as usual, a plentiful supply of shkootawahboo, or fire-water, had been provided, and indulging a hope that they would be enabled to have a pleasing drunken frolic. They landed and walked around the ground a few minutes; and discovering that the Indians were happily engaged in singing in different parts of the ground, looked on with astonishment, and curiosity was awakened to inquire what these things meant? They brought up their cloth tent and erected it near the gate leading to the river, at some distance from the other camps. Here they sat in surprise to see all the people sober.

"Having come from the south shores of Lake Huron, they had never heard the Word of Life; and when the horn sounded from the preacher's stand, they gathered with the people and took their seats in the congregation. Here they, for the first time, heard the name of Jesus. The Gospel proved the power of God. Their darkened minds were brought to see the exceeding sinfulness of sin; and while their souls groaned under the burden thereof, they were pointed to the Lamb of God. They sought His face during the prayer-meeting, which continued through the night; and before the morning broke forth to dispel its gloom, their guilt and darkness fled away before the Sun of Righteousness, and the man and his wife were made to rejoice in God their Saviour. The two first

7

days were very favorable. The weather was fine, although the nights were rather cool. After this we were drenched in rain by one of the heaviest showers I have experienced in this part of the country; and although I had endeavored to use every precaution to make our tents water-proof, such was the impetuosity of the torrent, that it poured in streams through the roof during the night. The preacher's tent, I had flattered myself, would prove a safe retreat for my brethren in the ministry, but on lighting a candle as the shower abated, and repairing thither, I found they were all in a woeful plight. Brother Lord was screwed up into a corner, snugly wrapped in a wet blanket, while his bed and pillows gave full proof that he was on board a leaky vessel. Our brethren Lunn and Fisher, from Montreal, had partaken largely of the cooling shower, and their appearance forcibly reminded me of a device I have somewhere seen, of "Patience on a monument smiling at Grief," when I saw them seated with their garments saturated with water, proving the contrast between a rainy camp-meeting in the woods, and the snug retreat of a citizen in his comfortable mansion in Montreal. The General Superintendent of Missions, Bro. Stinson, appeared determined to brave it out; for he lay amidst the roaring of thunder and the pouring of the water, rolled in the blankets, of which he appeared to have collected his full share, and seemed to be muttering in his woolly retreat, "Blow, winds, and crack your cheeks." On overhauling his blankets to discover his true situation, he observed he was wet but warm, and lay still, as though resolved to make the best of it. The morning exhibited an amusing scene. One might be seen hunting for dry linen, another drying his shirt, with a blanket thrown around his shoulders; sheets, blankets, etc., were spread on the bushes, and the most unequivocal testimony was given that our tents had been everything but water-tight. As I have heard no complaints from our brethren, I humbly trust they experienced no indisposition from this their camp-meeting excursion; and happy should I be to meet them again on the same spot, even under the same circumstances.

"The following evening presenting threatening indications of another shower, and our brethren not having entirely divested themselves of those symptoms of hydrophobia which succeeded the last night's ducking, thankfully accepted of an offer made by an American friend—crossed the river and spent the night, no doubt much more comfortably than they could possibly have done amongst our wet sheets and blankets. Thirty-nine tents were erected on the ground, two by our brethren from Baldoon, on the Thames Circuit, and two from the American side of the St. Clair; the remainder were occupied by Indians. About two hundred and fifty Indians were present, not one of whom left the ground without tasting that the Lord was gracious. A man and his wife, who lived some miles down the river, ventured to visit the spot. This pagan Indian had sent a message to us only a week or two previous to the meeting, saying, "I will surely kill you both as soon as I meet with you," meaning the missionary and the interpreter; but here the love of God was shed abroad in his heart, and he exclaimed, "How great a fool I was to talk of killing you, but I did not know that this religion was so good. I now love you, and will try to listen to your words as long as I live." On Sunday the Holy Sacrament was administered, and a profitable service it was—a time not to be forgotten. Twenty-two were dedicated to God in the ordinance of baptism, of whom, I may add, "they were all faithful." No case of backsliding has occurred as yet in this mission. One hundred and forty-three adults, with their children, have been baptized since last December, and I expect to administer the ordinance to about fifteen next Sunday, God willing. I have lately divided the converts into four classes, and appointed leaders from amongst the first who embraced the truth. They appear to do well, watch faithfully over their various charges, and promise to be useful men in the vineyard of the Lord.

"Our camp-meeting closed as usual by walking in procession around the ground, and shaking each other by the hand as a token of Christian friendship. This is effected by the preachers taking their stand as the procession walks around; and as each person passes, he shakes hands, and falls into the line next to the last person standing, so that when the last one in the procession comes, all on the ground have given each other the parting hand. And a solemn time for reflection it is; many part here to meet no more until they assemble before the judgment seat of Christ; and many are ready to say, having found true happiness during the services:

> "'My willing soul would stay
> In such a place as this;
> And sit and sing herself away
> To everlasting bliss.'
>
> "—J. E."

The following letter gives some of the results of Christian labor amongst the Indians on the River St. Clair. It was published in the New York *Christian Advocate and Journal:*

"ST. CLAIR, *June 27th*, 1837.

"From a desire to aid in the extension of the Redeemer's kingdom I venture to give you a little information. Being stationed by the Canada Conference at the St. Clair, I have not considered it beyond the sphere of my labors to visit occasionally the pagan Indians on the American side of the St. Clair River and Lake Huron; and I would state, to the glory of God and for the encouragement of His people, that many appear disposed to embrace Christianity. One opening I desire, through you, to make known to the Committee of the Missionary Society of the M. E. Church, viz., at Sahgeenong—on the map Sagenah—a large bay on Lake Huron.

"Three of the tribe of Indians known by the name of Sahgeenong Indians have embraced the truth at St. Clair, and remain with us at present, but would gladly return should their people become Christians.

"I have just returned from visiting the Indians assembled at Malden, U.C., where we found about one thousand. We spoke to many of them, but the ones I have alluded to I consider as especially worthy of notice.

"I called on the head chief at his tent, and explained to him our intention in coming to Malden, viz., to tell them of the Christian religion. He immediately summoned the other chiefs, and after counselling less than five minutes, they came together in the centre of the encampment and told us they would hear us. The young men and women stood around while we informed them of the spread of Christianity among the Indians, the improvements made among them, the benefits of schools to their children, and preached unto them Jesus; after which the chief arose and spake as follows:

"'I, with the chiefs seated around me, am very glad to hear that our Indian people are becoming better men. We acknowledge that we are very poor, and that the prospects of our children are cut off by the whites settling on our hunting grounds, and we know they must know more than their fathers would they live by-and-by. We have never before heard these words, and perhaps we may never hear them again; but we thank you very sincerely for the trouble you have taken in coming to tell us this time. We cannot comprehend the words you speak, because we know so little about these things, but we think your words are very good, and we should be glad to hear them again. Perhaps the next time we can understand them better.'

"The chiefs then came forward and shook us by the hand, thanking us for the 'good words,' as they expressed it. I told them that I would, if practicable, see them in company with some Christian Indians this fall; and, knowing the desire which animates the Church in your country to send the pagans the Word of life, I ventured to say, 'I think you will have a missionary and school teacher before a great while.'

"I give you herein a statement of facts which, if worthy of notice, will be taken into consideration. I most cheerfully and gratefully acknowledge that we, in our missionary efforts, have received much aid, in a pecuniary point of view, from our American brethren, and doubtless much divine influence in answer to their fervent and faithful petitions at the throne of grace; and could I in return in any measure aid in carrying into operation any plans, by the Committee adopted, for benefitting these Indians by establishing a mission or school, I should most gladly embrace an opportunity of so doing, so far as consistent with my appointed duties—at all times rejoicing that 'Methodism is one all over the world.' A good missionary and interpreter, ready to endure hardship and persevere under seeming impossibilities, would, I have no doubt, break up the ground, sow seed, and reap a harvest even in this hitherto barren waste. May the Lord direct!

"Since last December we have received 79 into the Christian community by baptism, and some now wait the administration of this ordinance. These are the first-fruits of St. Clair. May the God of missions extend His kingdom from the volcanic point to the

OLD FORT GARRY.

frozen regions, and in the full breadth of the land, until not a smoky wigwam shall want the Word of life nor a pagan's heart want the bread of heaven. If all pray thus, and all do something, soon will the wilderness bud and blossom as a rose, and this thirsty land become pools of water.

"I am, dear brother, yours in the Gospel of Christ,

"JAMES EVANS."

CHAPTER VIII.

EVANS' MISSIONARY LITERATURE.

JAMES EVANS possessed linguistic talent in an eminent degree, which was utilized on his fields of labor. Only the student of Indian languages can fully appreciate the work that he did, from the knowledge of the construction of the grammars of the languages, and the awkward manner in which all Europeans begin the study without a teacher. Every letter and particle is important, and none more significant than the particles incorporated in the verbs, as these are generally adverbs, prepositions, nouns and pronouns; besides they are inseparable in many instances, and cannot be dispensed with. The verb is the chief object of study in the language, and it is a formidable undertaking for the learner. Interpreters are hard to obtain sufficiently intelligent to translate accurately the ideas inherent in Biblical language.

By the comparative study of a few of the Indian languages, Evans was able to grasp intelligently their principles, and in a short time he began preaching in the Ojibway tongue, translating portions of the Bible and some Methodist hymns. That the translations might prove beneficial to the Indians and missionaries, a committee consisting of Revs. J. Stinson, Ephraim Evans, William Case, Peter Jones and James Evans was appointed to prepare and adopt a uniform system of orthography for the Ojibway language. Shortly after the Conference of 1837, Evans proceeded to New York with his translations, that he might have them printed. After some delay, the work was proceeded with, and satisfactorily completed. Peter Jones, on his return from England by way of New York, sought out the intrepid missionary, and mutual was the joy of meeting.

Nearly four months were spent in New York superintending the publication of the Ojibway translation, and then he homeward turned his weary feet, laden with literature for his red men.

A short time before going to New York he sent the following letter from the Credit Mission, where he was spending a few days arranging missionary matters, preparatory to going to Toronto, and then to New York.

"*July 4th*, 1837.

"Our Conference was peacable upon the whole, and closed with a very amicable feeling, and we trust the preachers went to their different fields of labor prepared to encounter and overcome the obstacles which presented themselves in the great work of preaching the everlasting Gospel. When Brother Hurlburt arrives he must take a house, if one can be procured in the village; and if not, he must rent one of the Indian houses. I am anxious the chapel should be progressing as early as possible, we must have a good house immediately. If anything can be done before I return, I shall be glad. We must go on with the subscription, and when the key is delivered £100 will be available from the funds of the Missionary Society. I expect you begin to think me rather long, but I think your patience will be more severely taxed before I return. I shall in all probability be absent yet about four weeks. I hope you will spare no pains in having the garden well cultivated. If you want a little money, you can get ten dollars from Mr. Moderwell, or Mr. Cameron if at home. I will remit you some before I leave for New York. Try to make yourself comfortable, and want for nothing; our circumstances are pretty good, and I shall be able to meet all demands without difficulty. Say to Wawanosh, that he will undoubtedly recover the Saugeen lands. The King wishes the Indians to keep every inch of land they own. The Conference have memorialized the Governor relative to the dissatisfaction of the Indians, and if he does not immediately grant the necessary relief, a committee is appointed, of which I am a member, to make application to the Home Government. A respectable and very influential society has been formed in England, of which some of the Royal Family are members, called the Society for the Protection of the Aboriginal Inhabitants of the British Dominions. Mr.

Egerton Ryerson is a member of the society, and will correspond on the subject of Indian grievances in this Province; and the day is not far distant when oppression shall cease, and our Indian brethren rise up to stand among us as men. They need only be faithful to God and He will do all things well. Write to me at New York when you receive this. My best respects to Brother Price; I will send his box. I hope he will continue in the school; his salary will be £25 and his board. This, I think, will make him comfortable. George had better try to remain till I return at least, when I think employment can be found for him. His salary will be the same as before, and I hope he will try and do something in translating some good tracts or other useful works."

After his hard toil in New York, with many annoyances and absent from his home very much longer than he expected, he wrote a cheery letter to his wife on the eve of his departure for home, which gives us an insight into his work, and reveals several pleasing traits in the missionary's character.

"NEW YORK, 10th *November*, 1837.

"MY DEAR WIFE AND CHILDREN,

"I this afternoon bid farewell to New York, and feel very much like giving them an English "One, two, three—hurrah!" My progress will not be very rapid homeward, as I have to see that all my goods pass through; for should one package be left on the way, it would spoil all my pains; I shall, therefore, accompany them. I have nine large boxes of books; seventeen boxes of stereotype plates of music; seven bundles of spelling books in sheets, and various other small ware, too numerous to mention. Two boxes and one bundle of paper I forward to Detroit by Buffalo, the others go to Toronto; should those sent by Detroit arrive before me, you will be kind enough either not to open them or to let any one see them, or to have anything to do with them, until I come. I hope to be home in ——, nay, I don't know ——, but, *now I am* coming. If any person asks any more, '*When?*' say, 'He's *coming*.'

"My spelling book has cost me $151 and a few cents printing; the hymns, $554.91, and the music $1,000, all of which, with my little bill of expenses here and travelling, will exceed a York sixpence. I'm as poor as a church mouse, but look to richer days. One thing I am sure of that you have been economical, *and so have I, it's true,* and very good reason, for I was seven or eight weeks with not twenty-five cents to spend. That was very providential, wasn't it? I'm as fat as a beaver, and as nimble as a deer. I am younger ten years than I was fifteen years ago; I long to be home to have a play with the children, the little girls and boys. Oh, by-the-by, don't forget Miss Jones (if such), give my ——; if mar — d, my respects. Let Clarissa oil the joints of the fingers of her left hand eleven times a day, so that they may be limber to beat me in playing the accordion. My buoyancy of spirits at starting for home has made me write as Shaungwaish says, a 'bely kulious letter.'

"My dear little girls, I kiss you both; be good girls, and try to make mamma happy, and when I come I'll make you all so. I shall not stay in Toronto any longer than is strictly necessary, perhaps two days, so that you may look for me about ——, by-and-by.

"I was extremely pleased and thankful to God to see George's letter in the *Guardian*, having not heard a word for about ten weeks; I ate it up like a hungry man. It gave me a special pleasure to hear that my dear people were faithful, and that their numbers were increasing. May God increase them more and more! I long to see you all. The paddles of the steamer will seem to move very slowly all the way; however, 'patience and perseverance overcome all obstacles."

"The next letter you receive, I expect to bring myself. I saw sister Verplank and Lily last night, and almost fancied I had my Clarry in New York; they send you a peck of love."

"May the Lord bless you all! Pray for me, that I may be brought in safety to 'my own fireside!'"

"Christian esteem to brother and sister Hurlburt, George and his wife and brother Price. Adieu! adieu! my dear wife and children. Your (during life) affectionate husband and father,

"JAMES EVANS.

"You must keep a good fire, as I shall be coming creeping in some evening very cold."

The man who could adapt himself to his surroundings so easily, was not to be annoyed with hard fare, as to food or sleeping accommodation; and this we find well illustrated in his trip to Toronto in the month of May, 1837, an account of which he gives in a letter written at Toronto, May 28th, 1837:

"After a tolerably pleasant passage of five days, I am safely in the vast metropolis of Upper Canada, where, through the mercy of God, I find all well. According to my resolution, I took deck passage on board the steamer *Buffalo*, and slept three nights on the softest plank I could select; by this means I contrived to reach Toronto, without having to stop to work on the road. On taking my passage, I flattered myself that I should, in my great blanket coat, pass through the voyage unrecognized, and that, consequently, my pride would not be wounded; but, behold, first came Mr. Orvis, of Black River, after we were on the way, 'How do you do, Mr. E.?' Next, the engineer, of whom I had no knowledge, asked, 'Elder, are you going to Buffalo?' And, to crown all, at dinner time a boy, who used to be cabin boy on board the *Gratriat*, came with, 'Elder, will you come to dinner?' I had the satisfaction of saying, 'Oh, I am a deck passenger!' At Cleveland, came on board a gentleman residing near the Credit, who very soon recognized me, and congratulated himself, saying, 'I am very glad to find I shall have some company;' and when the bell rang for breakfast, 'Come,' said he, 'we shall lose our seats.' 'I am a deck passenger,' said I; nor did I care one sou. Thus I had the chance of doing penance, and I hope it has done me no harm.

Although much pain of mind must be endured in taking a deck passage, by being compelled to hear a great deal of profane language, yet not more than would have to be endured in the cabin, where they are gambling and swearing half the night."

The missionaries on the new fields amongst the settlers, and on all the Indian missions, had to practise rigid economy; yet they were able to do so without compromising the dignity of their profession, or in any way injuring their social position. They lived respectably on small salaries, happy if souls were won for the Master. The riches of this world were forgotten in striving to lay up treasure in heaven. They had few books, but they mastered them, and thus became men of culture, able preachers and faithful pastors.

During a visit paid to Sarnia, in December, 1888, the writer learned from some aged residents of the town and country adjoining the St. Clair Indian reservation, who were friends of the earnest missionary during the St. Clair period of his work, that he was accustomed to cross the river to the American side to preach to the Indians who camped there. Clad in his blanket coat and moccasins he went to the wigwams, preaching the everlasting Gospel, praying with the sick, giving counsel in domestic affairs, and striving, by his faithful life and teaching, to overthrow the debasing customs of the medicine men, and to lead all the people into a nobler way of living. During one of his expeditions across the river to the Indian camps, he was suspected of being a Canadian spy, and was closely watched, if not arrested, for his expressed loyalty to the interests of the British crown. Ever zealous for the welfare of his Indians, he strove to lead them always to the cross of Christ, and had the satisfaction of seeing many rejoicing in the light, as the result of his ministrations. Large numbers were added to the Church while he resided on this mission, and very many of these remained faithful. The Rev. John Douse, who succeeded James Evans, wrote, a few months after he had gone to his field, a letter to his predecessor, in which he says:

"We have no drunken Indians. All is quiet among them; and their improved condition, their appearance and behaviour, speak much to your credit and success. God has highly honored you in their conversion and highly improved habits. I have seen no mission or people which I think equal to them. May you make yourself equally successful in your peculiarly difficult station. . . . . . Yesterday I read your letter to the Indians, who seemed glad to hear you talk to them, and about the prospects and Indians. I inquired if they had any word to send, and they replied, 'They were all great friends to you, and send their salute.' Here is one man who pretends to be a prophet—to have revelations and visions. 1. He says the people are not to attend class-meeting, as it would cause them to be lost; and not to go is the better way. 2. They are not to send their children to school, or to flog them, it will offend the Kezhe Munedoo. 3. That the Great Spirit is very angry with them for killing the large frogs which were found at the potato roots last fall, and it was very wrong, and will be visited with some judgment. 4. That the Great Spirit will save all who do right, though not Christians, and drink the firewaters sometimes. 5. Next spring he will preach, and the missionary and his interpreter will fall before him, and I suppose every one else. He has visited Ishpeming, and the bad place—been appointed of God a great prophet—and that another such prophet will be raised on Lake Superior, and two or three other places, in a year or two. I forget his name. The brethren generally think him a good man, but take little notice of his opinions. He is something of an Irvingite. My space will not allow of entering into further particulars. I am sorry to say he has drunk some whiskey, and pretends revelation to justify it. George Henry has preached against him."

The Rev. Dr. Evans, brother of the missionary, related an instance of the energy displayed in overcoming serious obstacles. The missionary had been engaged in church matters in Toronto, and returning homeward reached London, laden with stores for the family and mission, but found that not a single conveyance could be obtained to transport him and his baggage home. Squire Morrell, his host, urged him to remain for a short time, but duty compelled him to make preparations for his departure. He bought some siding and other material necessary to build a raft or skiff, and proceeded very ingeniously to construct one suitable for himself and his "traps." It was sided and decked over, leaving only a small compartment in which he could sit or kneel, and was made perfectly watertight. Stowing away his bedding, clothing, food and other articles under the decking, despite the remonstrances of his friends, he launched his tiny craft upon the turbulent waters of the swollen Thames.

Onward he sped, past drifting logs, sand bars, rocks and overhanging trees, guiding with a master-hand the destiny of his vessel, apparently heedless of the dangers and difficulties confronting him on his journey eager only to reach the goal where loving hearts anxiously awaited his return. Rapids, mill dams, and other obstacles of a more or less serious nature had to be overcome, but he bravely surmounted them all; for, trusting in the Master's care, he bore a charmed life, and, eager only to do God's will, he dared to strive to win. With paddle and sail he gladly journeyed on, "past where Kilworth and Delaware now flourish, through the Indian reservation at Muncey, circling the Big Bend; on past Moraviantown, through the embryo town of Chatham, past the great marshes circling Lake St. Clair, till he met the river of the same, when, turning up stream, he passed Walpole Island, until the high banks of Sarnia and home hove in sight."

Brave, skilful and pious, he safely reached his home, and in accents low and tender told anew of Jesus' love and the wonders of the Christian civilization he had lately enjoyed.

In 1833 the Rev. Egerton Ryerson was in England, negotiating for the union of the Canadian Methodists with the English Conference, and while there wrote a series of letters to the *Christian Guardian*, on "Impressions of Public Men and Parties in England," which aroused the ire of some of the Canadian politicians of that period. James Evans, with four other ministers of the Niagara District of the Methodist Church, sent in a protest to Dr. Ryerson, stating that they were anxious to have Canada freed from the trammels of a State Church, were loyal subjects of the Crown, and objecting to many of the statements made in the letters. Dr. Ryerson wrote to James Evans upon the matter, and a short controversy followed, but unity and love at last prevailed.

WINNIPEG IN 1871.

CHAPTER IX.

LAKE SUPERIOR.

THE fame of John Sunday and Peter Jones had spread far and wide, and the success of their ministrations had been witnessed in many Indian camps, so that many souls as far west as Lake Superior had heard the Gospel, and some had been constrained to give their lives to God. John Sunday had gone into their camps, and with tears in his eyes told the Indians of the saving power of the Cross of Christ, and the story of his mission had touched many hearts when with native eloquence he related it to Christian men and women at the missionary meetings. The Church became deeply aroused on the question, and resolved to carry on systematic labor on behalf of the red men, so in 1838 James Evans and Thomas Hurlburt were both taken from St. Clair and sent to toil in union in the district of Lake Superior. In a series of letters written by these worthy laborers at this time, we get glimpses of their life and labor, worthy of preservation and interesting to read. Impressed with the grave responsibility of the undertaking, burning with love for souls, and sustained by strong faith in God, they went forth boldly to engage in their work, singing with joy the Methodist pilgrim's song. Two men so fully equipped for the mission could not be found. Both of them were good linguists, had studied the grammatical construction of the Ojibway tongue, and were thoroughly conversant with the customs, habits and beliefs of the red men. Possessed of strong physical constitutions, willing to endure hardships, zealous in their Master's cause, anxious to see souls saved, determined at all hazards to succeed, and dreading no fear, they were suited to each other, and to the arduous undertaking which the Church had given them to do. The Christian people had confidence in the men, the power of the Gospel to save, and the anxiety of the natives to learn the way to life, so that they looked for success, and their prayers, sympathies and good wishes followed the missionaries on their westward trip. James Evans left his wife and children in Ontario, and proceeded to his mission, being preceded by Thomas Hurlburt and his wife. The following letter, addressed to Mrs. Evans, residing at Sarnia, reveals the strong feeling of loyalty to the British crown which was characteristic of the man.

"TORONTO, *June 8th*, 1838.

"MY DEAR,—I arrived safely in this city, through the mercy of Divine Providence, and found all well, excepting Charlotte, whom I found confined with small-pox; she has, however, had but a slight attack, and is now so far restored as to sit up, and begin to make a stir about the house.

"I received my dear Clarissa's letter, and was glad to hear of your health and the girls'. I was sorry to learn that George was not so well; but trust that God will speedily restore his health, and enable him, under the blessing of God, to devote himself wholly to the work of the ministry.

"I find all things peaceable in Toronto. You will see by the *Guardian* the burning of the *Sir Robert Peel* steamboat, one of the largest and best on Lake Ontario. There is certainly every prospect of war; and indeed it is inevitable, unless *Jonathan* will pay the piper. Lord Durham has arrived, and he speaks like a British peer; and while Gov. Marcy of New York, has offered 250 *cents!* oh, no! *dollars*, for the apprehension of the scoundrels, Durham says, 'I hereby offer £1,000 for each of the offenders, in order to assist the American authorities,' and should the gold fail in enabling them to make and keep peace and quietness, I guess as how Major Durham will be fixing out his rifle, and just kinder quietly sending a few fellows in red coats, with a few thousands of lead and iron justifiers of affairs, and by a thorough course of specie payment, settle in and balance the *Caroline*, *Peel*, Navy Island, and all other misunderstandings.

"We have enjoyed a very happy district meeting, our business has been transacted with the greatest unanimity of feeling and Christian affection. After the most mature deliberation, it was considered necessary for me to go to the Conference under the present state of Indian affairs. We have still stronger assurances that the Government at home are determined to do the Indians every justice, and to assist them as far as practicable, and I have no doubt but the doings of Sir F. will tend to help them rather than otherwise.

"Brother Hurlburt has obtained the consent of the district meeting to go to Mississippi; but whether the Conference will ratify the decision is a matter of doubt. We leave this on Monday, God willing. I shall be home as soon as possible, the time I cannot set. You may venture to arrange matters for my visit to the Manitoulin Island about the tenth of July; whether I go farther this year is rather a matter of doubt, and I should not be surprised if we are again stationed at St. Clair. I feel perfectly resigned to the leadings of Providence. God, who has hitherto directed our steps, is too wise to err and too good to be unkind, and I can say without a fear of the consequences, 'Where He appoints I go.'

"I met with Brother Chubb on my way to Buffalo, on his way from Keewawenong. He brought a letter from Ann's father, which Clarissa informs me you have received.

"I am glad to hear that he is satisfied. Brother Chubb says they do not intend to visit the Manitoulin this summer, so that I need not take Ann; but should her father be there, he can come down and see her I hope she is a good girl.

"I hope my dear baby is good, and endeavoring to improve in everything useful. Exchange kisses for me, and play 'Home, sweet home, there is nothing like home.'

"Say to Brother Price, nothing has been done respecting the school; but as soon as a teacher can be procured he will come on. I hope you have obtained the money from Mr. McGlashen and paid Mr. Davenport.

"Write me to Toronto as soon as you receive this, and I shall get the letter on my return from Conference.

"Say to the Indians by Brother Henry that I shall do all in my power to influence the Governor and Government in their favor, and that I hope they will industriously pursue the improvement of their lands, and strive to make their minds easy, and their families comfortable; and above all, remember that it is only by a dependence upon God, and obedience to His commandments, that they can expect His blessing. If they remain faithful, He will surely bless them; but if they forsake Him, He has said in His Word He will cast them off. They have many great and good friends both in America and England, and best of all is, God is their Friend. May God bless them and keep them in the path of light. . . . . . We left St. Clair on Tuesday morning, and had we not stopped at the Falls, we could have been in Toronto at five o'clock on Thursday evening, being about fifty-seven hours. We however stopped at the Falls until Friday, and arrived on Friday evening.

"My kind respects to Col. Thomson, Capt. Vidal and family, Messrs. Mothewell, Durand and lady, Jones and family, etc., etc., etc. May the Lord bless, preserve and keep you all.

"I am, my very extraordinarily dear and kind and never-to-be-forgotten, and more than all others beloved little wife, your indescribably affectionate and unchangeable husband,

"JAMES EVANS."

Never daunted by difficulties and dangers, but ever rejoicing in hope of better times, and laughing at impossibilities, he went on his way, assured by his fervent trust in God of the success of all his schemes. An extract from a letter dated July 17th, 1838, and written at Goderich, where he was tented at the mouth of the river, reveals his buoyancy of spirit which sustained him in trying times and places:

"DEAR WIFE AND WEANS,—Here I am, here am I. Now, I beg you won't cry, and I'll come by-and-by.

"We have been bungling along the lake shore as far as this place during the last four days; in fact, we've been dreadful lazy, but we are just waking up. We have been all preserved in good health and spirits, and have happened no more serious accident than just getting a wetting and cutting a little sort of a crack across the back of my hand; however, I have never allowed it to open, but shut it up with plaster, and it is no trouble to me, and I expect in a few days it will be well—at least, you must believe so, right or wrong.

"We had well nigh come back, when the north wind took us at the mouth of the river; however, we rowed on, and soon had a fine south breeze, which carried us within a few miles of Kettle Point, where we ran into a small creek, after scooping out the sand and forming ourselves a channel to enter. Here we camped very comfortably, looking southward, and my heart going pitter patter, and indeed, its been rattling against my ribs ever since I started. I feel a little better this morning. . . . . . . May God bless you all. I am as wet as a muskrat, and just starting out with a fair wind. Adieu! God bless you all! Kiss each other for me.

"And when I come back,
Which will be in a crack,
Then you'll each have a smack.

"J. EVANS."

The party continued on their journey, stopping at Manitoulin Island to preach to the natives. In a letter sent to his wife, who was residing at Cobourg, dated Mesezungeang, August 20th, 1838, he says:

"My last letter I finished at and forwarded from Munedoowauning (or Devil's Hole), the Indian name of the bay selected by Sir F. B. Head as the future residence of the Indian tribes; a very fit name, by-the-by. We arrived in this place on the 30th of July, all well, and immediately commenced endeavoring to do good, by preaching the blessed Gospel of salvation. The pagans have, during our stay, paid good attention I have no doubt but many have been favorably impressed with regard to Christianity. We have baptized several adults with their families, and left the island (Manitoulin) just two weeks after our arrival. We have not had fair winds, but fine weather during our passage to and stay on the Island."

WINNIPEG IN 1886.

On the 23rd of August, 1838, he wrote a letter from Sault Ste. Marie, as follows:—

"We, last evening, about five o'clock, reached this place after nine days' hard rowing, and one day's fair sailing. The blessed Lord has been very gracious to us, He has preserved us from all evil. We have not had a shower of rain to wet us since we left St. Clair, and we have never been laid by a whole day on account of heavy winds—we have all enjoyed good health—and our temporal wants have been bountifully supplied. In fact, our Munedoo provided for us when the Munedoos of the pagans let them hunger. I could particularize several instances, but one was so remarkable that it cannot be overlooked. Soon after our arrival at the Munnedoolin, Brother Sunday and his comrade came, and having neither money nor provisions, they turned in and shared with us in true Indian style the blessings which we were enjoying. Their company and our own made a family of ten, and all these mouths soon gave our flour barrel the consumption. On Saturday we found our flour and pork admonished us to be going, if we intended to have any provisions with us on our way to the Sault; and yet the presence of a Catholic bishop and two priests, together with Episcopal ministers, made it necessary that we should, if possible, prolong our visit. We, therefore, started out and peeled birch bark, and fished in the evening. A number of the Indians started out before us, and some at the same moment; some went down the bay, and others accompanied us upwards, not one who went with us caught a single fish. Their canoes ran within ten yards of ours for a mile or more, and fished ahead and astern of us, and caught nothing, but came home expressing the greatest astonishment on seeing that we brought home thirty-five pickerel. We told them the Lord sent them before the canoe, and I hope they believed it, for I am sure it can be accounted for in no other way. To His name be the praise for all our mercies; we have had plenty of fish, and we are now in the best fishing country perhaps in America. The Sault Ste. Marie is a very handsome place, and the people appear exceedingly friendly. It will surprise you when I say, that the waters of the St. Clair are muddy in the clearest time, compared with these waters; they are as pure as crystal, and teem with fish of the very first quality. The weather here is very fine, and I think at present as warm as in Toronto. I yesterday crossed the river and called on Mr. Nause, the Factor of the Honorable Hudson Bay Company; we found him, as we found the Agent's where I dated this letter, very obliging, and ready to render us every possible assistance in prosecuting our mission northward. He informs us, as do the principal traders in this vicinity who have travelled through our circuit, that there are abundance of Indians, more on the north shore than on the American side; but they are during the winter scattered on the mountains. However, there are many, whom the traders term 'Lake Indians,' who reside all winter near the shores; and we hope to succeed in inducing some of them to serve God, and thus open the way for access to a vast field of labor, and, as far as we have learned, every hope of success. You know, however, I am always sanguine, and my hope may arise as much or more from my natural disposition as from faith in the promises of God; however, I am endeavoring to trust His word, which says, 'Lo! I am with you always." There has gone up the lake this summer, a Mr. Cameron, a Baptist. He sends word down that the Indians are more attentive and more anxious to listen to the Gospel than any with whom he had met at any time. He is sent by the American Baptist Board. What a pity the Canadian and British societies cannot supply this region, without the Americans?"

James Evans' parents were residing at Charlotteville, Upper Canada, and as he continued westward he often thought of them in his times of hardship and want. Remaining for a short time at Mishibegwadoong, he addressed to them a letter from that place dated September 19th, in which he says:

"You may wonder why and how I wander about our vast wilderness, and I can assure you I am not less a subject of astonishment to myself. It is not from choice, for no man loves "home, sweet, home," more than myself, and I am happy in saying that no man's home is made more like home by those I love than is my own. But why do I talk about home; I have none—a poor wayfarer—and I must say, I thank God I can say it,

'I lodge awhile in tents below,
And gladly wander to and fro,
And smile at toil and pain.'

And why? I feel an answer within me. Because, 'Woe is me if I preach not the Gospel. . . . . Our prospects of success in prosecuting the great work to which the Church has appointed us, is at present flattering. We have met with many discouragements through reports of a discouraging nature, but God has graciously cleared away the mists which beclouded our atmosphere, and we find ourselves in a vast region of moral and spiritual darkness and degradation; but where the poor benighted heathens are already groping about to find some one to take them by the hand and lead them to the light. The Indians in this region are ready for the Gospel and anxious to be instructed, not as below, endeavoring to shun the missionary and standing aloof from his society, but seeking as diligently for us as we are for them. The few that are at home, at this post generally come in about the time of family prayer, in order to enjoy the season of worship with us; and we have this day learned that the Indians about Red River are coming six and seven hundred miles to inquire for missionaries. The Lord is indeed going before us and preparing the way, and our motto, through His grace, is 'Onward!' I shall not in any possibility find it practicable to return by next Conference, and shall do well if I get back next fall."

The devoted missionary can depict more fully and satisfactorily the details of missionary life than any writer who has not been on the field during the period, and knows little concerning the Indians of that region during those early years, and it is interesting to trace the record of his work, and the strivings of his spirit in his missionary toil. We shall, therefore, let him speak for himself, and enjoy the pen-and-ink sketches of his life. In a letter addressed to his wife and daughter, who were residing at Cobourg, dated February 10th, 1839, he says:

"You gave me a little paper class-meeting, and why should I not enjoy the same privilege? I am sure it will be agreeable to your feelings. Well I can, through grace, say that I am sure God has deepened His blessed work in my own soul since I arrived here. I enjoy great peace of mind. My intercourse with God is not clouded, but clear and satisfactory. I am endeavoring to seek after more of the mind which is in Christ. . . . . The world is losing its charms. I would just as soon be buried in the depth of these wilds as to be in a populous city. I love society, you know; but I trust that God knows I love the poor benighted heathen more, and heaven is just as near the wilderness as Toronto. I have no home but heaven, and I desire no other, but hope God will enable me to wander about these dark regions until He calls me home. . . . . I am not by any means unemployed here. I have a small school, and am striving to do all I can to advance both the temporal and spiritual interests of those among whom God has cast my lot this winter; but my sphere is rather limited. I hope as soon as navigation opens to get more open ground, and to find a more populous location for the future. Indeed, were it not I expect some help from Canada in the spring, I should leave this next month, and proceed on snow-shoes to Fort William. I very much regret not hearing from Brother Stinson this mail, as I cannot now expect to hear before May, and am something at a stand in my preparations for my next summer's route. Should I hear of war between Great Britain and the United States I shall be down to Conference, I think; but if not, not quite so early. You may, however, depend on my being down as soon as ever I can, consistent with the duties of my mission. These I must attend to, so long as I consider you safe; if otherwise, my duty is clear—to care for you first, next for the heathen."

When James Evans was stationed on the St. Clair Mission he had as his associate Thomas Hurlburt, and when he departed for the wilds of Lake Superior, the same devoted man accompanied him. This faithful missionary possessed linguistic talents of a high order, which enabled him in an incredibly short time to master the Ojibway language so thoroughly as to talk like a native. No other missionary of the Methodist Church has evinced such aptitude for grasping the intricacies of the Indian languages, the significant construction of the grammar, and the ability to converse freely in the native tongue of the people amongst whom he labored, as did this intrepid enthusiast of modern times. The testimony of the natives, corroborated by Peter Jones, supports this statement. Heedless of the dangers and hardships of the journey westward to Lake Superior, he took with him his family, and anxious only for the salvation of the natives and the glory of God, he entered the Indian camps, preaching Christ and Him crucified. The most thrilling tales of the devotion of the early Jesuit missionaries do not surpass the stories that might have been told of these missionaries amongst the Indians of the Lake Superior region. They only lacked the opportunity to seize the crown of martyrdom to exalt them as master missionaries and heroes among men. They had little time at their disposal to write long accounts of all their adventures, and they were too modest to relate their sufferings, whether for the sake of arousing in others like enthusiasm, or for the glory of God. Hurlburt had gone ahead of Evans and located at Fort William, where he had with characteristic energy begun his work. Under date of December 17th, 1838, he wrote a letter to James Evans, which reveals matters of interest to students of missionary literature:

"DEAR BROTHER,

"The mail arrived here last evening from Red River, and leaves to-morrow for the Sault; this is about two weeks sooner than we expected it. I arrived here on the 30th of October, just one week after leaving Michipicoton. With regard to my reception here, I have nothing further to wish. Mr. Swanston has done everything in his power to forward our objects and also to render me comfortable. Shortly after my arrival a house was prepared, and on the 6th of November I commenced school with twelve scholars; but after the return of the fishermen they increased to twenty. Their attendance is not regular, but it is very seldom that I have less than fifteen. As all speak the Indian here, I have the children repeat the Ten Commandments and Lord's Prayer. I sometimes explain the Commandments, and enforce the duties enjoined, and I am happy in hearing it observed that the children are more orderly than formerly. Upon my first arrival here, a request was made by some of the people, that I would have prayer with them every evening; though the majority are Roman Catholics, yet they pretty generally attend. When at home I generally have, perhaps, from thirty to fifty every night. My congregations on the Sabbath sometimes amount to as many as sixty. Whether we establish a mission here or not, I hope my residence among them this winter will do them no harm. There are six or seven Indian men here, and more women than men; the latter part of them attending on Sabbath and every evening to prayers and singing. (Mr. Swanston leads the singing.) The Indians here appear very fond of singing. Had I spelling-books and hymn-books, I could easily teach them to read the hymns. Four or five young women have attended school occasionally and having two spelling-books, I taught them nothing but the Indian. I am much pleased to see the facility with which the new orthography may be acquired by those uncorrupted with the old. I think that a month or six weeks' faithful application would enable a person entirely ignorant of letters to read the hymns with fluency. I shall not forget this thought if sent to any new mission in this country. When I take up a translation in another orthography, it makes me sick at heart to see the letters screwed, contorted and placed in every position to make them say something, and then you can give about as good a guess at the sound as though it was in Chinese characters. The chief of this place, Ashueoo (the Spaniard), who was baptized at the Manitoulin by the Rev. Mr. O'Neal, is now at the Grand Portage, or near there with the priest.

" This Ashueoo sent for the priest before he went to the Manitoulin, and since his return he has been baptized again by the priest. As soon after my arrival as convenient I endeavored to ascertain the true state of the Indians. I was sometimes told that all the Indians had been baptized by the priest, and again I would hear that only a part had. I can now reconcile these different accounts, for some of them remain constantly in the vicinity of the Fort, while the majority remain principally in the interior; and of these the better part have not been baptized by the priest, while the former have.

" I am at a loss what to say with regard to the prospects here; but am inclined to think that a mission might be established to advantage. The Catholics having got in before us is quite a drawback, and we shall have prejudices to contend with that had no existence a year or two ago. There is enough of good land here. Potatoes, barley, peas, oats and garden vegetables grow very well. Lake Nipegon and Rainy Lake are the two principal places in these parts for the resort of numbers of Indians. In my opinion, we should take these two places in preference to any others. Lake Nipegon is better situated for obtaining supplies of provisions than Rainy Lake. You will require a guide in going to Nepigon, as the river is not followed on account of being very rapid; but they go up a small stream, and carry over again to the main one. When you see the Governor you will, of course, make all necessary arrangements with him, should we think of occupying Rainy Lake and Lake Nepigon. I suppose it would be difficult for us to subsist for the first few years without assistance from the Company."

Thomas Hurlburt encountered many difficulties in his missionary toil, arising from antagonistic missions and the nomadic habits of the natives. His own particular work was hindered by the influence of a missionary named Cameron, whose father resided among the Indians at Michipicoton, where he had married the sister of the principal chief. The missionary claimed the Michipicoton Indians, and as he could speak the Indian language perfectly, his mother being an Indian, he had unbounded influence among the people. Despite these hindrances Thomas Hurlburt continued in labors abundant, and good results flowed from his disinterested toil.

In a letter addressed to James Evans, dated at Fort William, February 1st, 1839, he says:

"DEAR BROTHER,

"We expect the mail will arrive from the west next week, so I wish to be prepared for it in time, and not be taken by surprise, as I was before. I feel rather at a loss for materials to write an interesting letter, as there has been almost a perfect sameness in every respect since my arrival here. I am still in the school. I have preaching every Sunday, and prayers every night. I am much pleased with the attention paid by the people to divine things, though mostly members of the Catholic persuasion. I visit the Indians at their own homes occasionally, and they visit me every evening. I find them anxious to be instructed in religious matters, but their prejudices are so much warped in favor of the Catholics that it is difficult to deal with them as they might be dealt with. They have received the crucifix, beads, and other mummeries from the priest, instead of the Gospel, and to these they trust in the same manner as they formerly did to their medicine bag. My aim in every discourse is to show them, as they can bear, what the nature of true religion is. Some appear to be quite serious."

We shall get some further knowledge of the work and its difficulties from the pen of the same devoted missionary, which will give us an insight into missionary life, characteristic of the man. On April 9th,

EDMONTON.

1839, he sent from Fort William another letter to James Evans:

"DEAR BROTHER,

"Yours of the 24th of February I received on the 28th, and the one of the 25th of March arrived last night. Since writing my last there has been change enough to furnish materials for writing, if these changes were of sufficient importance to command attention. About the time of sending off my last letter, the priest at the Grand Portage became acquainted with the fact of my being here, and sent word prohibiting any of the members of his Church attending to my instruction. Shortly after, he sent an Indian, whom he has been instructing for some time, who came and remained until he had exacted a promise from all whom the priest could influence, that they would attend me no more. From what I learn from the Indians, the priest has been giving them his own version of a history of the Church. I need not tell you what this is. Seeing he commenced without any provocation, I thought it incumbent on me to say something in my own defence, or leave the impression on the minds of these ignorant people that I was convicted of being an agent of Mujemunetoo, and had nothing to say for myself. I requested that, as they had attended to me all winter, and had left me without giving any notice, they would come once more, as I had something to say to them by way of parting advice, but none came, they were so terrified by the denunciations of the priest and by a book which he sent, with the devil pictured in it, with a pitchfork throwing the Protestants into Tophet. The priest may get pay for this. Let him answer it. Before this my prospects were good, several I thought were seriously impressed, and I have since learned that one of the two that were here, that had not been baptized by the priest, had come to the conclusion to join himself to me; but, unfortunately for him, he applied for counsel in a wrong quarter.

"I have seen a few of the Indians of the interior, as they came to get their supplies. One of them, while here for a few days, attended the Indian priest, and also attended to hear me, and at going away he came and told me that he was pleased with what he had heard from me; that I was not like the priest, speaking evil of others, but what I said was good. He thanked me for my instructions. I am persuaded that some few might be gathered here yet; but their number would be small, as the priest and Mr. Cameron were among the band before I came. All, without exception, tell me that, had I come a year ago, they all would have joined themselves to me. I think that some one should be sent to Rainy Lake as soon as possible, before the priests do us more harm. I hear that Mr. Charles, the gentleman in charge, is anxious for a missionary, but says that he must have an inexhaustible supply of patience and perseverance to deal with those Indians. Mr. Taylor, at Nipegon, heard of my being here, and said he wished I was at Nipegon. The way is open for us in every direction. Had I an Indian with me, I should go to Rainy Lake for the summer. From what I hear of their character, I should expect them to be indifferent and shy at first. I heard that some of the Nipegon Indians said, 'What do we want of a minister, we have our own way?' Polygamy will be one great obstacle in our way at Rainy and Nipegon lakes. My impression is that one should teach our converts to read our hymns and sing them without any delay, as it will strengthen them greatly, and give them much consequence in the eyes of their pagan brethren ; and this is easily done.

"I stand ready for any part of the work. I want that you should write to me or Brother Stinson, or both, that it may be known at Conference what your arrangements are. Did I have the shaping of my own course, I should get James Young and go to Rainy Lake. I think to offer myself to the Conference for that field if I hear nothing from you; but I am willing to go anywhere, however remote and insignificant the place may be. If I get no word from you at the Conference, I can at the Sault on my return, and can direct my course accordingly. You, of course, know the situation of the Indians at the Peak; there has been no missionary to them yet. The Peak (pic) would be a comfortable situation for a man that had a family, as every necessary could be easily procured. I wish to go where God directs; that is all my wish!

"I intended to tell you that I had not written to Brother Stinson; but it slipped my mind at the time of writing.

"My little son, whom I never saw, made but a transient stay in this world on his way to a better. He died on the 18th of October, aged two months and seven days. My family were well up to the 9th of November. My wife had rather go with me across the Rocky Mountains, and live in a bark wigwam, on fish, than in a city full of kind friends and all the luxuries of life without me. We will see if her courage holds out when put to the test, in this Lake or Rainy Lake."

James Evans was assisted in his work by Peter Jacobs and his wife, Ojibway Indians, who had become sincere Christians. The winter and spring months of 1838-39 were spent in earnest missionary toil in the small camps of the Indians, but despite the solitude and poverty, the faith of the cross and the full assurance that God's will was being done, gave the conquest over all hindrances, difficulties and pain of body or mind. The sad intelligence was conveyed to the lonely missionary in the wilds of the west that his brother Joseph had been drowned. During the spring months Thomas Hurlburt bade adieu for a short time to his trying field of toil, and went east to attend Conference, where he elicited much interest and enthusiasm by his devotion to his mission, and the presentation of his Indian grammar and translations. After the Conference he returned to the west and spent several years among the Indians on the north shore of Superior, doing very effective work in educating the young, and leading souls to Christ, studying the languages of the people, and introducing many reforms in their domestic and social life.

James Evans did not arrive until after Conference, but was stationed at Guelph, Ontario, during 1839, whither he went in August of that year, and remained until he left for his great work among the Indians in the Hudson's Bay territory. A very successful year was spent at Guelph, where he showed such energy, sterling piety, and excellent preaching ability, that the people admired his talents, and he left a hallowed influence that has remained until the present time. The membership of the church in that place had an addition of sixty-four during that year. On this field he bade a long farewell to ministerial work among the white settlers, and henceforth devoted his time and talents to the elevation of the red race upon the lakes, prairies and forests of the great Northland.

TRAVELLING IN THE FAR NORTH.

CHAPTER X.

HUDSON'S BAY.

FIFTY years ago Western Canada was peopled by Indians and half-breeds and a few white settlers. The population was sparse indeed, for the country owned by the Hudson's Bay Company was several hundreds of miles in extent, and the weary traveller, in some parts of this vast territory, might travel two and three hundred miles without meeting a kindred soul. Indeed, settlers' homes were rare. The trappers and traders congregated in small groups, and built a "fort" of logs for protection against the roving bands of Indians. A country larger than Great Britain, France, Spain, Germany and Italy combined was inhabited by the Indians, half-breeds and traders, and not a soul cared to turn his eyes towards this land to make a home and spend his days therein. The city of Winnipeg stands midway between the Atlantic and Pacific Oceans, the eastern and western boundaries of the Dominion; and away westward for more than a thousand miles, and northward for nearly the same distance, the hunters roamed the plains and forests to procure furs for the Company's posts, and thither went the thousands of Blackfeet, Bloods, Piegans, Crees, Saulteaux, Kootanies, Sarcees, Chippewayans, and many other Indian tribes.

Toward this vast territory, in the year 1832, the Methodist Church was eagerly looking, wishing and praying that something might be done for the tens of thousands of red men that might lead them to live for righteousness and God. It was not, however, until the spring of 1840 that any decisive action was taken, and then it was British Methodism that wished to claim this land for Christ. The authorities of British Methodism, through the Rev. Dr. Alder, the Missionary Secretary residing in London, England, and the Rev. James Stinson, President of the Conference in Canada, informed James Evans that three young men were being sent from England to engage in mission work among the Indians in the Hudson's Bay Territory, and they wished him to take charge of the work in that country. He consented, and became General Superintendent of these missions. The Rev. Messrs. G. Barnley, W. Mason and R. T. Rundle embarked at Liverpool by the *Sheridan*, for New York, on the 16th of March, on their way to the territory of the Honorable the Hudson's Bay Company, to commence missionary operations among the settlers and native tribes of that vast region of North America, under the protection and chiefly at the expense of the Company, whose proposals to the Society have been of the most liberal and honorable character."* On the 12th of April, 1840, these young missionaries arrived at New York.† Without any specific arrangements being made, the intrepid missionary speedily completed all the necessary preparations for the journey to the northern land, and accompanied by his wife and daughter Euphemia, he started for Montreal to take passage, if possible, in the Hudson's Bay Company's brigade of canoes. He took with him two young Ojibway Indians, Peter Jacobs and Henry B. Steinhauer, as assistants in the work. These young men were the fruits of Indian mission work, and having received a good education, were well adapted for the mission field; and the General Superintendent exhibited good judgment when he made this selection. When he reached Montreal he found that the canoe brigade had gone, so we find him on May 12th, 1840, on board the steamer *Rideau* on the Rideau canal, going by the lakes and rivers to his destination. He met one of the young missionaries, "a fine fellow," at Lachine, the others having gone by the canoes. He proceeded on his journey, going by way of Sarnia, Detroit, Lake Huron, and into Lake Superior to Fort William without entering a canoe, but from this point they went by canoe, and found the

* "Wesleyan Missionary Notices," April, 1840.

† "Wesleyan Missionary Notices," July, 1840.

route tedious but interesting. He had to send his goods to London, England, to be sent to the Hudson's Bay, where they would arrive in three or four months after he had sent them. The Hudson's Bay Company had engaged to furnish the missionaries with all necessaries, as canoes, provisions, interpreters and houses free of charge, and letters of introduction to the factors in charge of the Company's "forts" had been given, so that they were well supplied with ways and means for their work.*

Burning with enthusiasm, and strong in faith and hope, he said, "I am in high spirits, and expect to see many of the poor savages converted to God." His destination was Norway House, but his field was of very wide extent, as he had the supervision of the whole work; and he rejoiced in the prospect of seeing the Pacific Ocean, for one of the young men was to be located at Rocky Mountain House, and it was his duty to visit him.

In the Minutes of the Conference for 1840, the mission stations were thus printed:

Norway House—Lake Winnipeg—James Evans.
Moose Factory and Abittibe—George Barnley.
Lac-la-Pluie and Fort Alexander—William Mason.
Edmonton and Rocky Mountain House--Joseph Rundle.

JAMES EVANS,
General Superintendent.

* "Case and His Cotemporaries," Vol. IV., p. 277.

The name of Mr. Rundle is changed in the Minutes of succeeding years, but when the writer was attending missionary meetings in Ontario, during the winter of 1888-9, he met in Toronto the faithful missionary of the North-West, the Rev. Thomas Woolsey, who is brother-in-law to Mr. Rundle, who stated that the name in full should be Robert Terrill Rundle. At the English Wesleyan Conference of 1887, the aged missionary Rundle was superannuated, thus closing practically the official labors of a devoted servant of God. All honor to these pious men, who amid poverty, sickness and isolation continued their arduous labors, heedless of the cold, undeterred by the lethargy of the Indians on religious matters as taught by Christians, or the threats of the bold bad men of the camp, and who at last, in the solitude of their homes, pray for the blessing of God to rest upon the red men of the Canadian North-West. Norway House, the headquarters of Evans' missionary enterprise, was founded in 1819, by a party of Norwegians who established themselves at Norway Point, having been driven in 1814-15 from the Red River.*

It became one of the chief depots of the Hudson's Bay Company, and was called Norway House. It is situated at the north end of Lake Winnipeg, and is nearly four hundred miles north from the city of

* "Franklin's Narrative," I., p. 61. Bouchette's "British Dominion," I., p. 41. Quoted by "Bancroft," Vol. 32, page 725.

EGERTON R. YOUNG.

Winnipeg. The fort was built at the mouth of a small stream called Jack River, upon a rocky foundation, hidden between the rocks which rise abruptly, so that the occupant of the canoe guided by the flag that floats from a staff erected upon a lofty eminence, cannot see the fort until he has nearly touched the wharf.* Near the fort lay the tranquil waters of Playgreen Lake, and between this and the fort rose a rugged mass of rocks, always covered with human beings when the canoe brigade arrived. Norway House was an excellent location for a mission, and especially for the General Superintendent, as the brigade of boats from York Factory and Red River, on their way to Athabasca and Mackenzie River, passed Norway House going and returning, thus the red man and half-breeds from widely scattered regions of the great North-West heard the Gospel and carried to their homes the truths and influences of the Christian religion. Nearly all the Indian tribes of the country were represented in these canoes, and the progress made from year to year on this mission was reported in the camps of the Indians in the far north, in the lodges of the prairie tribes of the great Saskatchewan, and from thence the story was carried by the warlike buffalo hunters to the busy camps of the Indians on the banks of the Missouri and Yellowstone.

* Ballantyne's "Hudson Bay," p. 116.

Robert Terrill Rundle arrived at Norway House in the summer of 1840, on his way to Edmonton, where he was destined to labor, and two very pleasant and profitable months were spent there. The Company's agent, Mr. Ross, and his amiable family, entertained him, a place of worship within the stockade was placed at his disposal, and contributions were freely given to help on the work. Seventy-nine baptisms and eight marriages were performed by this faithful man by the first of August, and the nucleus of a church formed.

James Evans arrived at Norway House in the first week in August, just two months after the arrival of Rundle.* He perceived at once the importance of the situation, and lost no time in laying foundations broad and solid upon which to rear a superstructure that would endure. The people among whom he had located were Crees, a tribe of Algonquin origin, allied to the Ojibways, Micmacs, Bloods, Piegans and Blackfeet.

Compared with other Indian tribes, they were an energetic race. They lived in a cold, bracing climate, where timber and water were in abundance. Far from the broad prairies, where the buffalo roamed in thousands, hunted by the Blackfeet, Sioux, Gros Ventres, Crows, Mandans and other Indian tribes, they

* Rev. John Semmens' MSS., "Methodism in Winnipeg District.

trapped beaver in the streams, fished in the lakes, pursued the moose, elk, foxes, and other wild animals which abode in the north land in endless variety, their flesh furnishing food for the hungry, and the extra skins being used as barter for other necessaries of life. Medium in height, thin and wiry, they were quick to perceive anything belonging to Indian life, were true and faithful guides, could run long distances without fatigue, and endure the pangs of hunger with apparently greater fortitude than the white man. They were a people intensely devoted to their native religion, seeing their gods in the sun, moon and stars, in the strangely shaped stones that lay in their path, the old, weird-looking trees that grew by the river's side, and the cliff or mound that skirted the lake. Superstitious were they to a great degree, having listened by the lodge-fires to the traditions recited by the medicine men and the aged warriors, and seeing as they fully believed, answers to their prayers every day. The influence of the medicine men prevented the people from indulging any hopes of finding the way of life from foreign sources, and when men and women learned to follow the teachings of the Christ, they soon found all the imprecations of the old conjurors brought down upon their heads. Evans' previous training enabled him to begin work at once, intelligently and with acceptance. His first winter was spent at the fort, instructing the people and studying the language.

In the following spring he resolved to locate his mission at some distance from the fort, as the influence of the population there was not conducive to the interests of religion. A beautiful island in Playgreen

NORWAY HOUSE FORT.

Lake, about two miles from the Norway House fort, was chosen, and there the mission was permanently located.* Donald Ross was the chief factor in charge of the fort, and from the inception of the work a strong friendship sprang up between the missionary and the Ross family. The new mission was called Rossville, in honor of its kind benefactor.

* Ryerson's "Hudson's Bay," p. 88.

The missionary went into the bush and, aided by the Indians, prepared the material for all necessary buildings. In a very short period a neat church, school and parsonage were erected, whose white walls contrasted favorably with the sombre shades of the tall trees in the background, and about twenty Indian houses were soon built, which were occupied by young and middle-aged men with their families.*

In the summer the Rossville Indians spent their time successfully in raising farm produce and in the winter they went off on their hunting expeditions.

So soon as the work was commenced, a school was opened, which was filled with merry boys and girls, who were taught reading, writing, arithmetic and singing by the missionary. Evans was a good musician, and proved successful in teaching the Crees to sing the songs of Zion, which they did in a very touching manner. The tunes the Indians learn from the missionaries become changed after a short period, retaining the substance of the tunes, with Indian variations. The children became proficient in their studies under the able management of Evans. R. M. Ballantyne relates in a very entertaining manner, a Christmas school festival which he attended, presided over by James Evans, in those early days. It was such an entertainment as had never been given, except by the mission-

* Ballantyne's "Hudson's Bay," p. 145.

ary, consisting of puddings, pies, and cakes, vegetables and venison, singing, recitations in English and Indian and religious exercises.* The enthusiasm and devotion of the missionary won the hearts of the men and women, and they rallied around him, listening to his words and striving to follow his example. The preaching of the Gospel brought conviction to their souls, and the tears trickled down cheeks unaccustomed to feel the effects of weeping. In the public services in the church on Sunday, and at the other religious services, souls were stricken down with fear, or aroused to a sense of responsibility, and at the altar of mercy they sought and found pardon to their guilty souls. Classes were formed and leaders appointed to care for the weak. The Indians in the camps heard of the good work; how their friends were discarding the medicine man's incantations, the gambling feasts, the war dances, the religious dances, and were rejoicing in the knowledge of sins forgiven, and from the lodges in the forest the people came to see for themselves. The work spread rapidly, so that the new converts began to tell with accents sweet of their new-found joy. All their hearts went out toward the tribes in the regions beyond.

Evans determined to visit the tribes who had not heard the sound of the Gospel, and, in answer to the

* Ballantyne's "Hudson's Bay," pp. 142-148.

promptings of his own heart, the importunity of some of the Hudson's Bay Company employees, and the entreaties of the Indians, he travelled toward the west. With his wonderful train of dogs, so fierce and swift, he sped over the snow hundreds of miles to the Indian camps and the Hudson Bay Company's posts, proclaiming Christ and Him crucified, and marking out fields for future laborers. Away to Oxford House, two hundred and fifty miles distant, then to York Factory, Nelson House, Moose Lake, Cumberland House, Isle-a-la-Crosse, Fort Perry, Fort Chippewayan, Fort Pitt, and away into Athabasca he goes, visiting Lesser Slave Lake and Dunvegan.*

Burning with a holy zeal for the souls of men, and never daunted by hardship or danger, he faced storms of the severest kind, that he might do the will of God. His journeys were long, and oftentimes very trying, yet he failed not to pursue his course and to win. Over the rivers and lakes he journeyed in his tin canoe, made out of sheet tin, which the Indians christened, because of its flashing brightness, *The Island of Light.* Gliding swiftly in this ingenious conveyance, as his well-trained crew propelled it through the waters by means of their strong paddles, he won the admiration of all the people, white and red.†

* Rev. John Semmens' MSS., "Methodism in the Winnipeg District."

† Rev. E. R. Young, in *Methodist Magazine.*

ROSSVILLE INDIAN MISSION IN 1854.

This missionary adventurer planted far and wide the banner of the Cross, and many souls were led by him to trust in the Christian Master of Life. When hundreds of miles from home, he sent letters to his wife written upon birch-bark. He bore a charmed life in that north land, for as he "ran" the swiftest and wildest rapids, crossed the lakes in the severest storms and travelled in the coldest weather, though oftentimes in danger, he always reached home at last.

CHAPTER XI.

THE SYLLABIC SYSTEM OF THE CREE LANGUAGE.

THE Cree Confederacy is one of the largest branches of the great family of Indians called Algonquin. In books written during the early period of the history of our country the people were named Knistineux and Kristineux, but for several decades they have been known under the simpler term, which is now universally used. They occupy a vast extent of territory, embracing at the present time principally Athabasca, Saskatchewan, Alberta, Assiniboia, Manitoba and Keewatin. Among the Indians there are distinctive names applied to the tribes by the people themselves, and not in use among the white people.

The members of the Blackfoot Confederacy use as a national appellation, Netsepoye, which means, the people that speak the same language; and the Cree national distinction is, Naheyowuk, the exact people.

Judging from the grammatical construction of their language, its harmony and beauty, and the influence it has exerted over the other languages, the Crees have a righteous title to their significant name. Invariably among the tribes inhabiting the North-West. some persons will be found who are able to converse in the

Cree language. Like all languages during the early stage of their development, it is agglutinative in form and like Indian languages in general, the entire language becomes a language of verbs. There are two leading dialects of this tongue, the Wood Cree and the Plain Cree. Differences of pronunciation are manifest among the tribes using the language, induced no, doubt, by separation, the influences of religion, population and local surroundings. There are few sounds in use, and consequently few letters are needed to give expression to them. Sexual gender is not denoted; but instead there are two forms employed, namely, animate and inanimate, referring to things with and without life.

There are two numbers, singular and plural, and in the latter there is a distinction peculiar to Indian language, namely, two first persons plural, the one including the first and third persons, and the other, first and second persons only; as Notawenan, our father, and Kotawenan, our father.

In the formation of names, the terminations in general reveal the class to which they belong. Thus abstract nouns end in *win*, simulative nouns in *kan*.

Nouns referring to water end in *kume*, and those denoting abundance have their termination in *skau*.

Diminutive nouns are formed by adding *is* or *sis*, as iskweo, a woman, iskwesis a girl.

The verb has seven conjugations, with a very elaborate display of moods and tenses, and a large number of different kinds of verbs. Many new words have been adopted from the English language, and after being thoroughly Indianized, have become incorporated in the Cree tongue.* When James Evans had got settled down to his work, he began with his accustomed energy to study the Cree language, conscious of the increased influence wielded by the missionary when able to speak to the natives in their own tongue. He found two efficient and willing helpers in Mr. and Mrs. Ross, the factor and his wife. An old Hudson's Bay employee who went to Norway House nearly fifty years ago, informed the writer that Mrs. Ross rendered the chief help to the missionary in studying the language. It was a comparatively easy task for James Evans to master the Cree tongue, as he was thoroughly conversant with the Ojibway language, and as these belonged to the Algonquin family of languages, their grammatical construction was similar. Possessing this advantage added to his natural aptitude for studying philology, he was not long in gaining knowledge sufficient to enable him to carry on a short conversation, and with the help of an interpreter, translate accurately and with force portions of the Scriptures and hymns.

* "The Indians; their Manners and Customs," p. 253. By the Writer.

Quick to observe the principles of language, and ever desirous of utilizing his knowledge for the benefit of others, he beheld with joy the recurrence of certain vowel sounds, which when fully grasped might prove of great service in simplifying language and preparing a literature for the people. The wandering bands of Indians which visited Norway House aroused the sympathies of the missionary, and he longed for some method by which he could send to distant camps of red men the knowledge of Christ and His salvation. Pondering deeply, working meanwhile and praying to the Most High for assistance, at last in the year 1841, the Cree syllabic system was completed, the alphabet distributed among the Indians, and placed in the school, and instruction given in its arrangement. In less than one year from his advent to Norway House, he had devised and perfected the syllabic system upon which his enduring fame rests. The syllabic system is based upon the principles of the system of phonetics. There are no silent letters, and each syllable is represented by a single character, which characters when combined make up words. In the Cree language there are four principal vowel sounds, as follows: ā, ē, o, ä, which in Evan's alphabet are represented by characters called *initials* or *primals*. The consonantal sounds are represented by characters called *syllables*, *syllabics* or *combinations*, and these are combinations of the vowels mentioned above with the following consonants, k, m, n, p, s, t, y, ch. There are also characters called *finals*,* *appendages*† or *terminals*,‡ which are used as terminations to the syllables, and thus occupy positions in the formation of words. These terminations are written at the top of the characters with which they are connected, and in smaller form than the syllabics proper. The harmonious and complete Cree language is written accurately by the Evans Syllabic System, which includes in its alphabet less than fifty characters, which can be mastered by any intelligent white man in less than an hour. This wonderful invention is represented completely in the following syllabic alphabet:

* Archdeacon J. A. McKay, "Psalms and Hymns in the Language of the Cree Indians."

† "Cree Hymn Book," by Rev. John McDougall and Rev. E. B. Glass, B.A.

‡ 'Methodism in Winnipeg District," (MSS.) By Rev. John Semmens.

THE SYLLABIC CHARACTERS.

I. INITIALS OR PRIMALS.

ᐁ	ᐃ	ᐅ	ᐊ
ā	ē	ō	ä

II. SYLLABICS.

ᐯ	ᐱ	ᐳ	ᐸ
pā	pē	pō	pä
ᑌ	ᑎ	ᑐ	ᑕ
tā	tē	tō	tä
ᒉ	ᒋ	ᒍ	ᒐ
chā	chē	chō	chä
ᑫ	ᑭ	ᑯ	ᑲ
kā	kē	kō	kä
ᒣ	ᒥ	ᒧ	ᒪ
mā	mē	mō	mä
ᓀ	ᓂ	ᓄ	ᓇ
na	nē	nō	nä
ᓭ	ᓯ	ᓱ	ᓴ
sā	sē	sō	sä
ᔦ	ᔨ	ᔪ	ᔭ
yá	yē	yō	yä

III. FINALS OR TERMINALS.

ᐨ = m	ᐠ = k	ᐧ = w
ᐣ = n	ᑊ = p	ᕒ = r
ᐢ = s	ᐟ = t	ᓫ = l
ᐦ = h	ᐦ = aspirate	ᐤ = ow
	ᕽ = Christ	

EXAMPLES OF WORD FORMATION.

ᒪᓂᑐ = ma-nē-tō = spirit.

ᓂᐱ = nē pē = water.

ᓂᔭ = nē-ya = I.

ᑭᔭ = kē-ya = thou.

ᓂᐱᐣ = nē-pa-n = summer.

ᒣᑕᑕᐟ = mā-ta-ta-t = ten.

ᑫᓀᐯᐠ = kā-nā-pā-k = a snake.

When the invention had been made, the first thought was how to utilize it for the benefit of the Indians. There was no printing press, type or paper, and it was impossible to get any. Naturally enough, the Hudson's Bay Company officials objected to the introduction of a printing press, lest that mighty censor of modern times, the newspaper, should find a location within the domains of the Company, and a powerful antagonist to its interests arise. The missionary, ever fertile in resources, whittled his first type from blocks of wood with his pocket-knife, made ink from the soot of the chimney, and printed his first translations upon birch-bark. Afterward he made moulds, and taking the lead from the tea chests, and old bullets, cast his first leaden type from these. In January, 1889, the writer called upon the Rev. Dr. Evans of London, Ontario, who informed him that his brother, before leaving Norway House for England, burned nearly all his manuscripts. Dr. Evans was in England in 1841, attending missionary meetings under the auspices of the Wesleyan Missionary Society, when a letter came from his brother from Norway House with rough castings of the Cree syllabic characters. The letter asked the Wesleyan Missionary Society to call on the Hudson's Bay Company authorities to obtain permission to have a printing press sent into their territory. Dr. Evans worked hard in conjunction with Drs. Alder and Elijah Hoole, to secure this permission, and a press and font of type were sent to James Evans. These were allowed to go into the country after Dr. Evans and the missionary authorities had given a pledge that the materials would not be used for any purpose but religious instruction. The aged minister has now in his possession in his home in London, Ontario, some of the original type made by James Evans, from tea lead and bullets. He has also some old books made of birch-bark, and others made of paper, printed in the Cree syllabic characters, and bound by the inventor himself.

In a letter written by Dr. Evans to Dr. Carroll, he refers to his brother's work at this time in its relation to the Hudson's Bay Company, and his invention, as follows :*

"You know his entrance into, and untiring prosecution of missionary work in the vast territory of the Hudson's Bay Company, and some of its grand results. The peculiar difficulties and painful trials which he had there to encounter will never be fully known, nor the wonderful triumphs which he achieved.

"His fearless spirit, resolute self-denial, and power of endurance were matters of astonishment to the traders and *voyageurs* of that vast region.

"I was told by factors and agents of the Company, when in British Columbia, who had known him in the great Saskatchewan country, that he was famed for unflinching courage, sometimes approaching recklessness, in running rapids which were always shunned by both white men and Indians. To save time in reaching his destination was with him a cardinal duty.

"Natural courage, combined with unshaken confidence in God, enabled him to achieve wonders in his lengthened journeys. While much respected and aided by most of the Company's officers, he had to encounter much opposition from some of them in regard to Sabbath observance, which he always enjoined upon the Indians, both at their homes and in his lengthened journeys by canoe and dog-sled. The day was a veri-

* *Canadian Methodist Magazine*, Vol. XVI., p. 337.

table day of rest. In several instances, he purposely started for distant points simultaneously with the Company's brigades, and always succeeded in reaching the destination before the brigades which travelled on the Sabbath ; and this, nothwithstanding the odds against him in the Company's choice of their best and most experienced *voyageurs*. During the visit of Sir George Simpson, the then governor of the Territory, the powerful influence of that gentleman was strongly arrayed against him on the Sabbath question. Sir George fearing that the resting on that day, by the many Indians and others in their employment, would injuriously affect the Company's interests. James Evans went down to Fort Garry, met Sir George and the Council, and contended several hours for the right of the Indians to enjoy the rest. In answer to threats that any who disobeyed the Company's orders, should have no access to the stores, and should be deprived of ammunition for their hunting purposes, he told the governor that if such measures were resorted to, the whole matter would be brought before the Aborigines' Protection Society in England, and, by petition, before the Queen and Parliament. The contest was warm, but the truth prevailed.

"You know his great success in the invention of the characters in which the Cree language is now written and printed. For some years permission to introduce types and a press was refused, but he labored on, casting leaden blocks from the lining of the chests in which tea was brought into the country, and whittling them into shape as best he could; and by a rough, improvised press of his own manufacture, succeeded in printing many hymns, sections of the Holy Scriptures, and primary school books, which were of great service. I was in England, in 1841, when a set of his home-made types was received by the Wesleyan Missionary Society, and took some part with them in obtaining permission from the directors of the Hudson's Bay Company to have a font cast, and, with a press, sent out to Norway House, pledges being given that they would be used only for mission work. Their arrival was cause of great joy and thanksgiving to God."

Mrs. Evans devoted much of her time toward helping the Indian women and girls, and acted as assistant compositor, aiding the missionary in printing hymns and portions of Scripture for the use of the Indians.

The invention was in a very short period understood by the Indians, who were able to master it in a few days. The writer has heard Steinhauer and Young repeatedly state that a clever Indian, on being shown the characters in the morning, was able to read the Bible by their use before the sun went down the same day, and that one week was all that was necessary for the average Indian to master thoroughly all the characters, and to use them accurately. A careful writer like Semmens has said that, "One month was all the time considered necessary to enable even the dullest to read for himself, the words of life and liberty." The following examples will show the method by which the single characters are united in the formation of words, and the general principles of the construction of the systems.

SPECIMENS OF THE SYLLABIC SYSTEM.

THE LORD'S PRAYER.

ᑲᑎᐯᔨᐦᒋᑫᐟ ᐅᑕᔭᒥᐦᐊᐤᐃᐧᐣ

ᓄᑕᓈᐣ ᑭᐦᒋᑭᓯᑯᕽ ᐁᐊᔮᔨᐣ, ᑭᑕᑭᔅᑌᔨᐦᑖᑲᐧᐣ ᑭᐃᐧᐦᐅᐃᐧᐣ;

ᑭᑐᑌᓈᐃᐧᐃᐧᐣ ᑭᑕᐃᐧᐅᒥᐦᒋᐸᔨᐤ; ᐁᐃᑌᔨᐦᑕᒪ ᑕᐃᐧᐃᐦᑭᐣ ᐅᑕ ᐊᔅᑮᕽ ᑲᐃᓯ ᐃᐦᑭᕽ ᑭᓯᑯᕽ.

ᒥᔮᓈᐣ ᐊᓄᐦᐨ ᑲᑭᓯᑲᐠ ᑫ ᐅᐦᒋ ᐱᒪᑎᓯᔮᕽ.

ᐁᑲᐃᐧᔭ ᐱᓯᔅᑫᔨᐦᑕ ᓂᒪᒋᑐ ᑕᒍᐃᐧᓃᓈᓇ, ᑫ ᐃᓯ ᐁᑲ ᐱᓯᔅᑫ ᔨᐦᑕᒧ ᑲᒪᒋᑐᑕᑯᐃᐧᔭᐠ;

ᒪᒥᔫᓃᓂᓈᐣ ᑭᒋᐁᑲᒪᒋᑐᑕᒫᕽ; ᐸᒋᑎᓴᐦᐊᒫᐃᐧᓈᐣ ᑲᒫᔭᑕᕽ:

ᑮᔭ ᑭᑐᑌᓈᐃᐧᐃᐧᐣ, ᒥᓇ ᓱᐦᑳᑎᓯᐃᐧᐣ, ᒥᓇ ᑭᐦᒐᔨᐃᐧᐃᐧᐣ, ᑲᑭᑫ, ᒥᓇ ᑲᑭᑫᐧ ᐁᒣᐣ.

THE TEN COMMANDMENTS.

ᑲᒥᑕᐦᑕᐦᑎᐦᑭ ᐃᐧᔭᐢᐁᐧᐃᐧᐣᐊ.

---

1 (ᐯᔭᐠ) ᓇᒪᐃᐧᔭ ᐊᐃᐧᔭᐠ ᐱᑐᐢ ᒪᓇᑐᐊᐧᐠ ᑭᑲᐊᔮ-
ᐊᐧᐗᐧᐠ ᐃᐢᐱᐨ ᓂᔭ.

2 (ᓂᓱ) ᓇᒪᐃᐧᔭ ᑲᐅᓯᐦᑕᐧᓱᐣ ᑫᑳ: ᓇᐢᐱᓯᐦᒋᑲᐣ ᐊᐦᐳ
ᑲᑕᓇᐢᐱᑕ ᒧᒪᑲᕽ ᐱᑯ ᑫᑳ: ᑲᐋᐧᐠ ᐃᐢᐱᒥᕽ ᐊᐦᐳ ᑳᐊᔮᐠ
ᐊᐢᑮᕽ ᑕᐸᓯᐢ ᐊᐟᐳ ᑳᐊᔮᐠ ᓂᐱᕽ ᓯᐸ ᐊᐢᑭᕽ ᓇᒪᐃᐧᔭ
ᑲᐸ ᐱᐢᑖᐧᐊᐧᐠ ᐊᐟᐳ ᐸᒦᐢᑖᐊᐋᐧᐠ; ᐊᐃᐢ ᓂᔭ ᑲᑎᐯᓭᒋᑫᐠ
ᑭᒪᓂᑐᐡ, ᓂᑲᕽᐁᐧ ᓭᑕᐢᑭᐣ ᐁᒪᓂᑐᐃᐧᔭᐣ. ᐁᐸᑭᑎᓇᒍᐊᐧᑲᐧᐤ
ᐅᐅᐧᓯᓴᐠ ᐅᐊᐧᓂ ᑐᑕᒍᐃᐧᓂᓭᐤ ᐅᐦᑕᐃᐧᐋᐧᐊᐧᐠ ᐃᐢᑯ ᓂᐢᑕᐧᐤ
ᒥᓇ ᓄᐅᐧᐤ ᐊᐣᐊᐢᑲᐨ ᑲᓅᐦᑕᐃᐧᑭᒋᐠ ᑕᐦᑐ ᑳᐸᑳᐧᓯᒋᐠ. ᒥᓇ
ᐁᓄᑯᐦᑐᐊᐧᑲᐧᐤ ᑭᓴᐊᐧᑎᓯᐃᐧᐣ ᐅᑭᐦᒋᒥᑕᐦᑐᒥᑕᓇᐁᐧᐊᐧᐠ ᑕᐦᑐ
ᑲᓵᑭᐦᐃᒋᐠ ᒥᓇ ᑲᑲᓈᐁᐧᓭᐦᑕᐦᑭᐠ ᓂ ᐠᔭᐢᐁᐧᐃᐧᓇ.

3. (ᓂᐢᑐ) ᓇᒪᐃᐧᔭ ᐱᑲᐧᐣᐃᑕ ᑭᑲᐅᑎᓄᐣ ᐅᐃᐦᐅᐃᐧᐣ
ᑲᑎᐯᓭᐦᒋᑫᐟ ᑭᒪᓂᑐᐡ, ᐊᐃᐢ ᑲᑎᐯ ᓭᐦᑫᐟ ᑭᑕᑕᐡᐁᓭᒣᐤ
ᐱᑲᐧᐣᐃᑕ ᑫᐅᐟᑎᓇᐡᐃᓭᐟ ᐅᐦᐃᐧ ᐦᐅᐃᐧᐣ.

4 (ᓀᐅ) ᑲᓇᐁᐧᓭᐦᑕ ᐊᔭᒥᐦᐁᐃᐧ ᑭᓯᑲᐤ ᑭᑲᓇᒋᐦᑕᓭᐣ
ᑲ ᐃᓯ ᐃᐧᔭᐢᐋᐧᑎᒼ ᑲᑎᐯᓭᐦᒋᑫᐟ ᑭᒪᓂᑐᐡ. ᓂᑯᑕᐧᓯᐠ
ᑭᓯᑲᐤ ᑭᑲᐊᑐᐢᑳᐣ ᒥᓇ ᑭᑲᑐᑌᐣ ᑲᐦᑭᔭᐤ ᑭᑕᑐᐢᑫᐃᐧᐣ; ᒪᑲ
ᑌᐸᑯᐦᐦᐦ ᑕᑐ ᑭᓯᑳᐠ ᐁᐊᐧᑯ ᐅᑕᓭᐁᐧᐱ ᑭᓯᑲᐡ ᑲᑎ ᐯᓭᐦᒋᑫᐟ
ᑭᒪᓂᑐᐡ; ᐁᑯᑕ ᓇᒪᑫᑳ: ᐊᑐᒼ ᑫᐃᐧᐣ ᑲᑐᑌᐣ ᑭᔭ, ᐊᐦᐳ
ᑭᑯᓯ, ᐊᐦᐳ ᑭᑕᓂᐢ ᐊᐦᐳ ᑭᓇᐯᐃᐧ ᐊᑐᐢᑫᔮᑲᐣ, ᐊᐦᐳ

ᑭᑎᐢᑫᐧᐃᐧ ᐊᑐᐢᑫᔩᑲᐣ ᐊᐦᐳ ᑭᒍᐢᑐᓯᑦ, ᐊᐦᐳ ᑭᓯᓯᐊᑎᒍᑦ, ᐊᐦᐳ ᐱᑯ ᐊᓇ ᑭᐱᓯᐢᑮᑦ ᐊᐦᐳ ᑲᒪᐣᑌᐃᐧᐟ ᐱᐦᒋ ᑭᑎᐢᑳᐦᑌᒥᕽ.

5 (ᓂᔭᓇᐣ) ᑭᐢᑌᔨᑦ ᑯᐦᑕᐃ ᒥᓇ ᑮᑳᐃᐧ ᑲ ᐃᓯ ᐃᐧᐊᐢᐋᐧᑎᐢ ᑲᑎᐯᔨᐦᑫᐟ ᑭᒪᓂᑐᑦ ᑭᑕ ᑭᐣᐅᐦᑖᕽ ᑭᑭᓯᑲᒫ, ᒥᓇ ᑭᑕᒥᔪᐸᔨᔭᐣ ᐃᑕ ᐊᐢᑮᕽ ᑲᐸᑭᑎᓂᐢ ᑳᑎᐯᔨᐦᒋᑫᐟ ᑭᒪᓂᑐᑦ.

6 (ᓂᑯᑕᐧᓯᐠ) ᓇᒪᐃᐧᔭ ᑭᑲᓂᐸᐦᑳᐣ.

7 (ᑌᐸᑯ‴) ᓇᒪᐃᐧᔭ ᑭᑲᒪᒪᐃᐧᐦ ᐃᑐᐣ.

8 (ᐊᔨᓇᓀᐤ) ᓇᒪᐃᐧᔭ ᑭᑲᑭᒪᑎᐣ.

9 (ᑫᑳ‾ᒥᑕᑕᐦ) ᓇᒪᐃᐧᔭ ᑭ· ᑭᐊᐢ ᑭᐊᒋᒪᐤ ᑭ‾ᐊᔨᓯᓂᐤ.

10 (ᒥᑕᑕ‴) ᓇᒍᐃᐧᔭ ᑭᑲᐊᑲᐋᐧᑕᒍ ᐋᐧᐤ ᑭ‾ᐊᔨᓯᓂᐤ ᐃᐧᐊᐧ; ᓇᒪᐃᐧᔭ ᑭᑲᐊᑲᐋᐧ ᑕᒍᐋᐧᐤ ᑭ‾ᐊᔨᓯᓂᐤ ᐅᐊᐧᐢᑲᐃᑲᐣ, ᐊᐳ ᐅᓂᐦᑖᐃᑭᒋᑲᐣ, ᐊᐦᐳ ᐅᓈᐯᐃᐧ ᐊᑐᐢᑫᔩᑲᐣ, ᐊᐦᐳ ᐅᑎᐢᑫᐧᐃᐧᐊᑐᐢᑫᔩᑲᐣ, ᐊᐦᐳ ᐅᓯᓯ‾ ᐊᑎᑦᐅᐢ, ᐊᐦᐳ ᐱᑯ ᑫᑳ ᑳᑎᐱᔭ ᐁᐃᐧᓯᐟ ᑭ‾ᐊᔨᓯᓂᐤ.

THE SWEET BY AND BYE.

ᐊᔨᓇᓀᐅᒥᑕᓂᐤ ᑌᐸᑯᐦᐳᓭᐟ.

---

1 ᐃᑕᑲᐧᐤ ᐁᒥᐊᐧᓯᐠ ᐊᐢᑭ
ᒪᑲᐧᐨ ᐊᐧᐦᔪᐤ ᑯᓭᐸᐦᑌᓇᐤ
ᒪᑲ ᑯᐦᑕᐃᐧᓇᐤ ᐁᑯᑌ
ᑭᐊᐧᐁᐧᔨᐢᑕᒫᑯᓈᓇᐤ.

ᐁᑯᑌ ᐹᑎᒫ
ᑭᑲᓇᑭᐢᑯᑖ ᑐᓇᓇᐤ
ᐁᑲᑌ. ᐸᑎᒫ
ᑭᑲᓇᑭᐢᑯᑖᑐᓇᓇᐤ.

2. ᑭᑲᓂᑲᒧᓇᐤ ᐁᑯᑌ
ᐱᒫᒋᐦᐅᐃᐧ ᓂᑲᒧᓇ
ᐊᐦᒍˣ ᒧᓭᐠ ᑕᒥᐁᐧᔨᒧ
ᓇᒪ ᐃᐦᑕᑲᐧᐤ ᓀᐤᑐᓯᐃᐧᐤ.

ᐁᑯᑌ ᐸᑎᒫ, &c.

3 ᑯᐦᑕᐃᐧᓇᐤ ᑭᑲᒥᔓᓇᐤ
ᓵᑭᐟᐟᑐᐃᐧ ᓇᓈᐢᑯᒧᐃᐧᐤ
ᐁᒥᔨᑯᔓˣ ᐯᒪᒋᐟᐁᐧᐟ
ᓭᐁᐧᔨᐦᑕˣ ᑕᐦᑐ ᑭᓯᑲᐤ.

ᐁᑯᑌ ᐸᑎᒪ, &c.

CHAPTER XII.

ROSSVILLE AND BEYOND.

THE knowledge of this wonderful invention was soon noised abroad among the Indian camps, and the fame of this great teacher, who had left his home to train the sons and daughters of the red men spread far and wide. In the lodges of the Crees, Saulteaux and other tribes of Indians, the people talked about the wonderful invention of the missionary at Norway House. The brigades of boats that passed to and fro carried the news far inland among the bands of heathen Indians, and soon at York Factory and Fort Garry it became known that a wise missionary had devised a very simple plan by which the Indians could in a few days read as well as the white man, who has spent some years learning to read and write. We need not wonder at the astonishment of the Indians and half-breeds, for the records of its influence and simplicity have aroused the interest and sympathy of men of culture, and not the least amongst the number, Lord Dufferin, late Governor-General, who, when the characters were explained to him by E. R. Young, said, " Why, Mr. Young, what a blessing to humanity is the man who invented that alphabet! I profess to be a kind of a literary man myself, and try to keep up my reading of what is going on, but I

INDIANS OF THE PRAIRIE.

never heard of this before. The fact is, the nation has given many a man a title, and a pension, and then a resting-place and a monument in Westminster

Abbey, who never did half so much for his fellow-creatures. Who did you say was the author or inventor of these characters?"

"The Rev. James Evans."

"Well, why is it I never heard of him before, I wonder?" and the missionary aptly replied, "Well, my lord, perhaps the reason why you never heard before of him was because he was a humble, modest Methodist preacher." "That may have been it," replied the courteous governor, and we agree with his decision.

The wonderful simplicity and adaptability of the system to the Indians' modes of thinking, the construction of the language and wants of the individual made it peculiarly attractive, and the knowledge of its existence rapidly spread. Although James Evans possessed superior intellectual powers, he was more at home in rugged missionary work than when engaged in purely mental toil. He looked for results, and whatever would ensure the salvation of souls and the civilization of the tribes was eagerly grasped and utilized for these purposes. His heart went out toward the inhabitants of the distant regions who had never heard the sound of the Gospel, but the people belonging to his particular mission claimed his first and most earnest attention.

Having found that there were many serious disadvantages toward successful missionary work by the close proximity of a white settlement to a mission, James Evans determined to remove his mission some distance from the fort. A spot was chosen about two miles from the Norway House Fort, and in honor of the factor, Donald Ross, who was of great service to the cause of Christianity, it was named Rossville. So soon as the selection of the location was made, the missionary went into the woods with the Indians and got out timber, and rapidly native houses were built, with bark roofs, displacing the skin lodge which was the ever-present evidence of nomadic habits. The village grew, until in a short time twenty native dwellings, besides the mission premises, were erected. The children were gathered into the school and taught, the women found efficient teachers and helpers in Mrs. Evans and family; and the missionary translated, printed the translations in the syllabic characters, and bound them with his own hands. During the period of which we write, R. M. Ballantyne, author of "Hudson Bay; or, Every-day Life in the wilds of North America," was a clerk at Norway house in the service of the Hudson's Bay Company, and in his book he has given an entertaining reminiscence, which fully illustrates missionary life at Rossville, which we must give the reader the pleasure of reading, as the famous author was a frequent visitor at the Rossville mission house.

"Mr. Evans, the Wesleyan missionary, is to give a feast to the Indians at Rossville, and afterwards to examine the little children who attend the village school. To this feast we are invited; so in the afternoon Mr. Cumming and I put on our moose-skin coats and snow-shoes, and set off for the village, about two miles distant from the fort. By the way Mr. Cumming related an adventure he had had while travelling through the country . . . Mr. Cumming concluded his story just as we arrived at the little bay, at the edge of which the Indian village is built.

From the spot where we stood the body of the village did not appear to much advantage, but the parsonage and church, which stood on a small mound, their white walls in strong contrast to the background of dark trees, had a fine picturesque effect. There were about twenty houses in the village, inhabited entirely by Indians, most of whom were young and middle-aged men. They spend their time in farming during the summer, and are successful in raising potatoes and a few other vegetables for their own use.

In winter they go into the woods to hunt fur-bearing animals, and also deer, but they never remain long absent from their homes. Mr. Evans resided among them and taught them and their childen writing and arithmetic, besides instructing them in the principles of Christianity. They often assembled in the school-house for prayer and sacred music, and attended divine service regularly in the church every Sunday. Mr. Evans, who was a good musician, had taught them to sing in parts, and it was a wonderfully pleasing effect upon a stranger to hear these dingy sons and daughters of the wilderness raising their melodious voices in harmony in praise of the Christian's God.

Upon our arrival at the village we were ushered into Mr. Evans' neat cottage, from the window of which is a fine view of Playgreen Lake, studded with small islands, stretching out to the horizon on the right, and a boundless wilderness of trees on the left. Here were collected the ladies and gentlemen of Norway House, and a number of indescribable personages, apparently engaged in mystic preparations for the approaching feast. It was with something like awe that I entered the school-room, and beheld two long rows of tables covered with puddings, pies, tarts, stews, hashes, and vegetables of all shapes, sizes and descriptions, smoking thereon. I feared for the Indians, although they can stand a great deal in the way of repletion; moderation being, of course, out of the question with such abundance of good things placed before them. A large shell was sounded after the manner of a bugle, and all the Indians of the village walked into the room and seated themselves, the women on the one side of the long tables, and the men on the other. Mr. Evans stood at the head and asked a blessing, and then commenced a work of demolition, the like of which has not been seen since the foundation of the world! The pies had strong crusts, but the knives were stronger; the paste was hard and the interior tough, but Indian teeth were harder and Indian jaws tougher; the dishes were gigantic, but the stomachs were capacious, so that ere long numerous skeletons and empty dishes alone graced the board. One old woman, of a dark-brown complexion, with glittering black eyes, and awfully long teeth, set up in the wholesale line, and demolished the viands so rapidly that those who sat beside her, fearing a dearth in the land, began to look angry; fortunately, however, she gave in suddenly, while in the middle of a venison pasty, and reclining languidly backward with a sweetly contented expression of countenance, while her breath came thickly through her half-opened mouth, she gently fell asleep, and thereby, much to her chagrin, lost the tea and cake which were served out soon afterwards by way of dessert. When the seniors had finished, the juveniles were admitted *en masse*, and they soon cleared away the remnants of the dinner.

"The dress of the Indians upon this occasion was

generally blue cloth capotes with hoods, scarlet or blue cloth leggings, quill-worked moccasins, and no caps. Some of them were dressed very funnily, and one or two of the oldest appeared in blue surtouts, which were very ill-made, and much too large for the wearers. The ladies had short gowns without plaits, cloth leggings of various colors, highly ornamented with beads, cotton handkerchiefs on their necks, and sometimes also on their heads. The boys and girls were just their seniors in miniature.

"After the youngsters had finished dinner, the schoolroom was cleared by the guests; benches were ranged along the entire room, excepting the upper end, where a table, with two large candlesticks at either end, served as a stage for the young actors. When all was arranged, the elder Indians seated themselves on the benches, while the boys and girls ranged themselves along the wall behind the table. Mr. Evans then began by causing a little boy about four years old to recite a long, comical piece of prose in English. Having been well drilled for weeks beforehand, he did it in the most laughable style. Then came forward four little girls, who kept up an animated philosophical discussion as to the difference of the days in the moon and on the earth. Then a bigger boy made a long speech in the Saulteaux language, at which the Indians laughed immensely, and with which the white people present (who did not understand a word of it) appeared to be greatly delighted, and laughed loudly too. Then the whole of the little band, upon a sign being given by Mr. Evans, burst at once into a really beautiful hymn, which was quite unexpected and, consequently, all the more gratifying. This concluded the examination, if I may so call it; and after a short prayer the Indians departed to their homes, highly delighted with their entertainment. Such was the Christmas feast at Rossville, and many a laugh it afforded us that night as we returned home across the frozen lake by the pale moonlight."

The zealous missionary could not rest contented with the work at his own mission, but began to project schemes for the salvation of the tribes beyond.

Long journeys were undertaken in the interests of the degraded tribes, and some of these, lasting several weeks, and in some instances months, were periods of hardship and toil, sweetened with the burning zeal which dwelt in his breast for the salvation of men.

The intense cold, scanty and hard fare, isolation and manual labor, were gladly endured for the sake of the men and women of the northern wilds, who, haunted with superstitious fears, wore their amulets to protect them from the power of their spiritual foes. The Christian songs of the crew of the missionary's canoe, touched the hearts of many of the savage red men, and they longed for the peace of mind revealed to them through the preaching of the truth of God. Many were the narrow escapes of the mission party in the dangerous rapids of the northern rivers; but, nerved by the example of their intrepid leader, they braved the greatest dangers for the glory of God and the souls of their fellow-men. Wonderful tales of the missionary's daring and love for the red men were told around the camp fires far away in the interior, and on toward the region of perpetual snow; and visitors occasionally came from distant camps inquiring the way of life. The village of Rossville rapidly improved, so that the school was better attended, and the children made rapid advancement in their studies. The missionary possessed musical talent, which he used to good purpose in training the people to sing, so that they were soon able to read music and sing their different parts in a very creditable manner. Small farms were cultivated, the women learned to spin and sew, and the men became handy in the use of hammer, saw and plane. Civilization made rapid strides when the people accepted the Gospel. They were taught that "Cleanliness is next to godliness," and the lessons taught were soon seen in better houses, cleanlier and neater homes, and happier hearts. James Evans gives us a glimpse of his work in 1844, in a letter, as follows:

"The Rossville settlement will this autumn consist of thirty dwellings, a church unfinished, a school-house, and a workshop. The timber of which the latter is built was all growing in the woods on Tuesday, and the building was completed by Saturday evening.

"No expense was incurred, as the Indians did all the work, the women supplying bark for the roof. . . Industry is advancing under the influence of Christianity. The field we have cultivated, gives promise from present appearances of abundant returns. We expect to harvest this year from four to five hundred bushels of barley, from eight hundred to one thousand bushels of potatoes, and about one hundred bushels of turnips. These are fair results of one year's planting, considering the climate, and the newness of the soil. In a year or two it is expected that the Indians will raise enough from the fields to keep themselves above want.

"The school under Thomas Hassel is prosperous. He is accomplished and diligent, and deserves my highest commendation. His qualifications, piety and unremitting labors, have induced me to grant him a local preacher's license. He is a Chippewayan by birth, but speaks quite fluently French, English and Cree.

"Our society consists of eleven classes, supplied with leaders and assistant leaders. There are in these one hundred and twenty-one members, whose piety and Christian deportment have called for no disciplinary interference since their conversion to Christianity. The school is attended by nearly sixty pupils, about half of whom read and write both English and Indian. The others are spelling and reading easy lessons.

Religious truth constitutes a large portion of their instruction, the Creed and the Lord's prayer, in both languages, are familiar to all of them, and our own catechisms are repeated by all the more advanced boys and girls. They are improving in their knowledge of arithmetic."

Rossville continues to improve under the care of the missionary, and the Christian Indians sought to imitate the "ways of the white men," in a few instances not to their advantage morally, nor to their physical comfort. For some years after the death of the devoted Evans, the mission rapidly waned, and the prospects were very dark, but in 1872, the regular congregation at Norway House was eight hundred, with a church membership of three hundred and fifty.*

Many important missions have sprung up at the places visited by Evans in the early days.

The work of translating proceeded well. James Evans had brought with him Henry B. Steinhauer, from Ontario, who was left at Fort Frances (Rainy Lake) as assistant to the Rev. William Mason, who was stationed at that place, and this young man was destined to do much for God and the Indians by translating the greater part of the Bible into the Cree language.†

The Toronto Globe, August 16, 1872.

†"The Indians—Their Manners and Customs," by the Writer, p. 244.

In 1842, Peter Jacobs, an Ojibway Indian and minister of the Methodist Church, was stationed at Norway House as assistant missionary; and in 1843, the Rev. William Mason was sent by the Conference of that year to Norway House, to be associated with James Evans. In this latter year the Rev. George Barnley was stationed at Moose Factory and Abittibe. Peter Jacobs went to Rainy Lake and Fort Alexander, and Robert T. Rundle was at Edmonton and Rocky Mountain House, all of the missions being under James Evans as General Snperintendent. The printing of books and tracts in the Cree syllabic was continued by James Evans and his helpers, with the aid of a press made by the missionary himself, which, however, was replaced by a press and type sent from England, which performed the work more speedily and perfectly. Mrs. Evans assisted in the work as compositor, and as soon as Mr. H. B. Steinhauer was transferred to Norway House, the work of translating the Scriptures into the language of the Cree Indians, and adapted to the syllabic systems was begun. Some of these translations were utilized during James Evans' residence at Rossville, having been begun and continued under his supervision.

Not, however, for some years afterward was the translation of the whole Bible completed. Mr Steinhauer having translated the Old Testament from

Job to Malachi inclusive, and the New from Acts to Revelation inclusive, and Mr. Sinclair having translated the other books of the Old and New Testaments. The writer has in his possession one of the original manuscript copies of Genesis in the Cree syllabic, which is a fine specimen of penmanship. Owing to the growth of the missionary work and the absence of James Evans from Rossville, on missionary trips, it was felt that assistance was needed, and Mason came in the summer of 1843. In the old baptismal register of Rainy Lake, there are recorded in the handwriting of the Rev. William Mason one hundred and fifty-two baptisms. All the persons were baptized by him, the first being:

Alexander, son of William and Mary Sinclair, aged five months, of Fort Frances, District of Lac la Pluie (Rainy Lake), performed in 1840, and the last:

Martha, daughter of Gebazonnaszung and Nundunmeg, of Lac la Pluie, and this ceremony was performed in 1842. The next baptism recorded was performed by the Rev. Peter Jacobs in 1843, and he exchanged places with the Rev. William Mason, Mr. Jacobs being transferred by the Conference of 1843 to Rainy Lake. The work was so arranged that one of the missionaries was at Rossville during the absence of the other, and in this manner was the work of the outlying missions carried on successfully. Oxford House, two hundred and fifty miles distant, was visited, and even the far distant Saskatchewan heard the sound of the Gospel from the lips of Evans. At Fort Edmonton, the devoted Robert Terrill Rundle preached the Gospel faithfully to the Cree and Stony Indians.

During the year 1845, he was residing within the Hudson's Bay Company's fort at Edmonton, when Paul Kane, author of "Wanderings of an Artist," met him, and received from him some assistance relative to journeyings in the Saskatchewan country. The artist has left some pleasant reminiscences of the zealous Rundle in his books upon the Indians.

Evans ever faithful in the discharge of his duty, reproving Indian and Englishman alike for their sins, heedless of the difference in their social positions, soon found opposition from those who had professed to be his friends. This, however, did not deter him from doing his duty, as he relied upon the power of the truth, the justice of his cause, and the help of God, and He prevailed; not in his own day, but in the latter days posterity has seen the truth triumphant and the character of the godly missionary fully vindicated.

OXFORD HOUSE MISSION IN 1854.

CHAPTER XIII.

HOME AT LAST.

AT the inception of the Norway House Mission James Evans met Sir George Simpson, the Governor of the Hudson's Bay Company, who received him with distinction and treated him with kindness. The establishment of Christian missions among the Indians was freely discussed, and the governor kindly offered his assistance in the maintenance of the missions. The missionaries were to hold the same rank as the wintering partners or commissioned officers of the Company; the same allowance was to be given them, and when going out on missionary expeditions, canoes or other conveyances were to be furnished free of expense. In return for these material aids it was stipulated that the missionaries should not, in any way, interfere with the natives, so as to injure the interests of the Company.* This seemed perfectly legitimate, and no reasonable man could object to such a pleasant arrangement.

Matters went on smoothly for a time. The canoes were furnished, and assistance was freely given to the

* "Twenty-five Years' Service in the Hudson's Bay Territory." By John McLean, Factor in Hudson's Bay Company. London, England, 1849.

missionaries whenever needed, so that in the early years the servants of the Company were useful assistants in all mission work. James Evans did not, however, intend that any arrangement should interfere with his declaration of the truth of God, and in the discharge of his duties toward his dusky parishioners there could not be any compromise with man.

When the natives and employees of the Company attended the religious gatherings, they were taught to revere the Sabbath day, and follow the teachings of the Bible. There was nothing, apparently, wrong in this, and, indeed, it was the only course open for him, but the rigid observance of these truths was the cause of a long course of opposition which ended disastrously indeed. When the Indians began to rejoice in the consciousness of salvation, they refused to work on the Sabbath, and although threats were used, these failed to compel them to break the divine law. Upon a few occasions white men in the employment of the Company refrained from working on the Sabbath, and these were reproved for wasting their time and injuring the interests of the Company.

James Evans sometimes travelled to distant posts, starting at the same time as the parties going from the forts, and by resting on the Sabbath while the others travelled, he always reached his destination first. Such evidences as this wrought powerfully upon the minds of the Indians, and the Christian converts steadily refused to toil on the Lord's Day. Sir George Simpson could not allow another master in the territory owned by the Company, and he chafed under the growing influence of the missionary who could win men to obey the laws of God. Gradually and quietly the assistance given to James Evans and his fellow-missionaries was withdrawn, and serious charges were made by the Indians and white people, at the instance of officials in the Company's service, assisted by one of the missionaries who, filled with jealousy, had joined hands with the conspirators, and, in a foul manner, sought to destroy the reputation of a true man.*

False witnesses were produced, who swore to the truth of the charges. In the meantime, the faithful missionary, careworn and sad, but brave and noble in the midst of his foes, continued his ministrations, reproving the careless, warning men of the impending wrath of God for the transgression of the divine laws, and his influence gradually widened by means of the syllabic system. He felt, however, that the work was in a precarious condition, besieged by friends and foes, but, trusting in God, he labored on, rejoicing in the power of the truth to save the souls of men. Determined to proceed to Athabaska on a missionary expedition, he went to the commander of the fort, and asked assistance, but this was refused.

* Twenty-five Years' Service in the Hudson's Bay Territory." By John McLean. London, Eng., 1849.

Taking with him Thomas Hassel, his faithful school teacher and interpreter, he set out for the Indian camps. This young man was a devoted Indian who became the constant companion of the missionary, ever ready to interpret the Gospel as it was preached to any band of Indians, willing to undergo any hardship for the sake of Christ, and able to translate hyms and portions of Scripture under the most trying circumstances. As they were crossing a small lake together, a flock of ducks flew overhead, and anxious to get a shot at them, James Evans drew out his gun, which lay under the seat of the canoe. In the act of doing so the gun was discharged, and its contents were lodged in faithful Hassel's breast, killing him instantaneously. With a heart full of sadness, and well-nigh distracted, the missionary returned to Rossville. Some of his friends advised him not to visit the relatives of the young man, or the band to which he belonged, as the Indian customs demanded compensation for the dead. Invariably the law was a scalp for a scalp, a life for a life, or their equivalent. Trusting in God, his own innocence, and the love of the Indians, he went to the young man's home, and related all the circumstances of the sad calamity, offering to become a son in the place of the deceased. By adoption into the family his life was preserved, but he never recovered from the blow. The Indians loved the man who had done so much for them, and who was ever anxious for their welfare, but his stern opposition to the use of intoxicating liquor among the Company's employees, as productive of great harm to the natives, begat opposition to him and his work. Strong influences were brought to bear against him, supported, and in some instances instigated, through the Governor, insomuch that some of the Indians testified against the man who sought to do them good. The faithful toiler, well-nigh heart-broken, was recalled, and at last the scene of his labors, where he had labored hard to to lay the foundation of purity and material progress, had to be forsaken. Sad were the days spent in preparation for his departure. Friends and foes shunned him, as one who had been guilty of crimes, for the officials of the Company had opposed him, and no loving heart or hands were stretched forth to help him in his hour of distress. Faithful servant of God, thou hast not labored in vain, nor art thou alone in thy sorrow and solitude! Blest companions of thy pain and isolation hast thou in the man of Uz; Savonarola, the martyr of Florence; Carey, in India; and the immortal dreamer of Bedford jail. Thy God shall defend thee, when foes are many and strong!

James Evans bade farewell to the northern land, so full of sacred memories, and so dear to his heart. It was there he had devised and perfected his syllabic system, and from the primitive mission house there had gone forth portions of the Word of Life, printed on the home-made printing-press, and bound with his own hands. From this centre of missionary influences the truth had spread, and now several hundreds of Indians were rejoicing in a consciousness of salvation. Many times had he stepped into his canoe and gone forth to tell the dusky sons and daughters of the forest, the good news of salvation through Christ, until he had listended with joy as the woods rang with the shouts of happy souls who had found the great Master of Life. A sad and long farewell, a weary journey to Eastern Canada, and then to England he sailed away. A thorough investigation was made relative to the charges which had been preferred against him, and in every instance he was declared innocent. Not a single charge was proven, and then were found out the organized efforts which had been put forth to tarnish the reputation of an honest man by foes and professed friends. He had no sooner reached the shores of England than a general demand was made for his services at missionary meetings. Although in feeble health, he gladly responded to the call, and was in labors more abundant. His stories of missionary life in the valleys of the Saskatchewan, along the rivers and in the forests of Keewatin and Athabaska, aroused the sympathy and love of the Christian people assembled at the missionary gatherings, and great was the joy of the churches because of the spread of the knowledge of Christ among men. His thrilling tales of missionary heroism and native devotion touched the hearts of many who wept for joy as they listened to this new romance of modern missions. These people had heard of Moffat's success in Africa, the story of Carey's devotion and linguistic labors in India, and Henry Martyn's zeal and consecration in Persia were familiar to their ears; but the salvation of the Cree Indians and the invention of the syllabic system was something new in missionary annals, and their delight was unbounded. Burning with love for his work, he spared not himself, although in feeble health, but in charming language and with holy eloquence he told anew the story of his life. A missionary meeting was held at Keilby, Lincolnshire, on November 23rd, 1846, attended by a large concourse of people, where he spoke on his much-loved theme, and after the meeting, having retired to his room he suddenly passed away from the land of pain and trouble to be forever with the Lord. In the Minutes of the British Conference of 1847, the following obituary was published relating to the man and his work:

"James Evans was a missionary of remarkable ability and zeal, and of great usefulness among the North American Indians. His success among the aborigines of Canada led to his appointment as General Superintendent of the recently formed missions in the Hudson's Bay Territory. To his mental vigor and indomitable perseverance the Indians are indebted for many advantages; among these is a written and printed character, suited to their language, of which Mr. Evans was the inventor. Many were the afflictions and trials he had to endure; these issued in a failure of health, which rendered his return home desirable, but the results were not favorable. He died suddenly at Keilby, in Lincolnshire, on the 23rd November, 1846, at the house of a friend, after attending a missionary meeting, at which his statements had excited great interest."

Thus lived and died James Evans, at the age of forty-six years. His years were not many, yet he lived long, for his work was great and enduring. Despite all the influences of opposition at work, the man still lives in the missions established, souls won for Christ, and the translations of God's Word. After the withdrawal of James Evans from Norway House, William Mason was left in charge of the Norway House Mission, and was stationed at Rossville. He remained there until the year 1854, when he left the Conference and united with the English Church. In July of that year he was ordained priest at Fort Garry by Bishop Anderson, and appointed to York Factory, whither he went in August.

Having been associated with Evans, Jacobs and Steinhauer for several years, he knew all the work which was engaged in by them, and became conversant with the Cree language, doing some good work among the Indians. Some time after, Mr. Mason went to England on a visit, and took with him the manuscript translations of the Bible which had been made by Steinhauer and Sinclair, which had been entrusted to him, and were to be printed by the British and Foreign Bible Society. When this work was finished, Mr. Mason allowed his name to be put upon the title-page as the translator of the Bible. It has also been claimed on behalf of Mason that he was the inventor of the Cree syllabic characters, and the writer has seen this claim put forth on his behalf through the columns of the religious press within the past three years. The claim, however, is at variance with the facts. Before William Mason had ever come in contact with the Northern Crees, and while he was still a missionary at Lac la Pluie, James Evans had sent to England specimens of the type which he had made himself, and also a few translations made in these characters. Some of these are still in existence, and in possession of the relatives of James Evans. Translations were made in the Cree syllabic characters in 1841, and a set of home-made types sent to England in that year, while William Mason did not go to Norway House until 1843. The writer has heard H. B. Steinhauer repeatedly tell the story of his translations when living with Evans and Mason at Norway House.

The testimony of the missionaries of the Roman Catholic and Protestant Churches, many of whom the writer has conversed with, is that Evans alone planned and perfected the syllabic system. Every writer of the early period asserts that Evans was the sole inventor. Ballantyne, in "Hudson Bay; or, Every-Day Life in the Wilds of North America," page 159, says: "In fine weather I used to visit my friend Mr. Evans, at Rossville, where I had always a hearty welcome. I remember on one occasion being obliged to beg the loan of a canoe from an Indian, and having a romantic paddle across part of Playgreen Lake. I had been offered a passage in a boat which was going to Rossville, but was not to return. Having nothing particular to do, however, at the time, I determined to take my chance of finding a return conveyance of some kind or other. In due time I arrived at the parsonage, where I spent a pleasant afternoon in sauntering about the village, and in admiring the rapidity and ease with which the Indian children could read and write the Indian language by means of a syllabic alphabet invented by their clergyman. The same gentleman afterwards made a set of leaden types, with no other instrument than a pen-knife, and printed a great many hymns in the Indian language."

The famous lady writer, Miss Tucker, better known as "A. L. O. E.," in her book, "The Rainbow of the

North," p. 257, published in 1851, while William Mason was still residing at York Factory, writes:

"During the Bishop's stay at York Fort four Indians applied for baptism. Two of them resided on the spot. They were half-brothers, and it appeared that one of them, who went by the name of John, had, four years before, visited Norway House, where he heard the Gospel preached by one of the Wesleyan missionaries. Anxious to know more, he procured a copy of the Cree alphabet, of which he soon made himself master; he then obtained a catechism in the same language, which, with indefatigable perseverance and by embracing every opportunity of help from others, he learnt to read. He communicated his knowledge to his brother Joseph, whose heart also was touched, and they were now both of them candidates for admission into the visible Church. The other two were also brothers; they came from Fort Churchill, 180 miles to the north of York Fort, and had, it seems, long ago received religious instruction from one of the Company's officers, Mr. Harding."

In a foot-note to the above, the authoress adds: "These were but rare, as the alphabet and catechism were in peculiar characters, invented by the late Mr. Evans, a Wesleyan missionary."

John McLean, a factor in the Hudson's Bay Company, and author of a book, "Twenty-five Years' Service in the Hudson's Bay Territory," and published in London, England, in the year 1849, states that Mr. Evans, "with his pen-knife cut the types, and formed the letters from musket bullets; he constructed a rude sort of press; and, aided by Mrs. Evans as compositor, he at length succeeded in printing prayers and hymns and passages of Scripture for the use of the Indians."

In a paper published in "The Proceedings of the Canadian Institute," page 166, October, 1889, the Rev. Father A. G. Morice, O.M.I., Stuart's Lake, B.C., in writing upon "The Western Dénés—Their Manners and Customs," says that in order to teach the Dénés to read and write their own language, "he has had to compose a syllabic alphabet somewhat on the principle of that so suitably invented by the late Mr. Evans for the Cree language; but which he soon found to be totally inadequate to render correctly the numerous and delicate sounds of the Déné dialects."

Since the early days of missionary work in the land of the Northern lights, an extensive literature in the syllabic characters has sprung up under the devoted labors of Protestant and Roman Catholic missionaries.*

Books of a religious nature have been translated by English Church missionaries and published in England, and several books have been translated by Methodist missionaries, which have been printed in England, but during the past year a font of type has been brought to Canada, and a hymn-book has been printed in the syllabic characters in Toronto. The

* "The Indians—Their Manners and Customs," pp. 255-258. By the Writer.

Roman Catholic missionaries have availed themselves of Evans' invention, and for many years translations have been printed in these characters. These books are silent teachers of truth to men and women in the Indian camps. The Bible in the syllabic has been exerting a powerful influence for good among the members of the vast constituency speaking the Cree language. Oftentimes Stony Indians have visited the Macleod mission house, occupied by the writer, and from under their blanket-coats they have drawn copies of the Bible, well thumbed, giving evidence of having been used to good purpose. Indians have found the way to peace through reading the books given to them by Christian Indians. Travelling bands of Indians have gone out on hunting expeditions hundreds of miles from their home, and seated beside the camp-fire have sung to their pagan brethren the songs of Zion, which have stirred deeply the hearts of their dusky friends. Then taking out their Cree books they have taught them how to read, so that without ever having seen a white teacher they have learned the story of the love of Christ. Far in the north a band of hunters met a pagan band of Indians who had never heard of Christ. They told them the wonderful story, and by means of the syllabic characters the pagans were in a short time enabled to read. The Christian Indians remained long enough with them to make them acquainted with the syllables, and then when they were parting the pagans begged for copies of the Word of God. Unable to comply with the request, and still anxious to help them in the way of life, they tore their Bibles into parts and divided them among the people.

A number of Indians called at the Rossville mission house during E. R. Young's residence there, seeking religious instruction. They had copies of the Great Book and were able to read it, but were not able to understand, so they had come a journey of thirteen nights that they might learn more about the Saviour of men. A copy of the Bible was shown them, which they read with perfect ease. They had never seen a missionary, and lived hundreds of miles from a mission house, still they were able to read the Bible. The Hudson's Bay Company's agent had some copies of the Bible in the Evans' syllabic characters, which they had seen, and obtained possession of. They visited a band of Christian Indians at a long distance from their own home, and from them they received help, so that they were soon able to read. So well pleased were they that they remained with the band for some time, and then they returned to tell the story they had heard to others. Thus, without any teacher or missionary, many of the Indians in the forest and along the rivers and lakes of that northern land have learned to read the Word of God for themselves. Some years after the death of James Evans, the Rev. Thomas Hurlburt (1857) was stationed at Norway House, and the old companion of the deceased missionary translated some tracts and utilized the printing press at Rossville in printing three thousand copies of a book comprising one of the Gospels and four of the Epistles. The stitching and binding was done by Miss Adams, the school teacher, and his pressman was an Eskimo. The syllabics have been used by the Indians as a means of correspondence, letters being written upon birch-bark.

Since the early days, mission work has been continued, and now Roman Catholic, English Church, Presbyterian and Methodist missionaries are laboring among the Cree Indians.

The Stony Indians read the Evans' syllabic characters and write them freely and neatly. Missionary work has brought peace and prosperity to the Indian tribes. Listen to the Christian songs that float upon the evening air as the aged chief leads the devotions of his family, and then the whole camp is resounding with the praises of God. Many of the privileged sons and daughters of Christian homes have been pricked to the heart when in that land of snow they have witnessed the devotion of the red men to the Christian's God and their love for the Bible.

Lord Southesk, who visited that country, says in his book, "Saskatchewan and the Rocky Mountains," page 250, "Our Stony messenger met us on the road, bringing me a letter from his people, written in the Cree syllabic characters. It was translated to me as follows:

"We thank God for sending us such a great man; we send our compliments to him; we will receive him as a brother." Again on page 259, he says:

"At night a bell was rung in the Assiniboine camp, and the Indians all joined in singing hymns, as they do every night. The service lasted some time. It was a sort of a chant, the men and women occasionally singing in parts. Their preacher is an aged and venerable man. He learned Christianity from another Indian, I believe, but his gift of preaching is entirely self-developed. Mr. Woolsey had since occasionally visited these people, who, as far as I could learn, are now well instructed in the Christian faith, and certainly carry out its precepts in their lives."

The Cree literature in the Evans' syllabics was an agent of peace during the rebellion in the North-West. When superstition, hatred and fear were stirring the hearts of the Indians in the valley of the Saskatchewan the native teachers of righteousness and the missionaries were counselling peace, and as the Indians read anew the Word of God, they determined to live at peace, and seek help from God. Shortly after the rebellion, when the three Indian chiefs—Pakan, Samson and Bear's Paw—visited Ontario under the guidance of Rev. John McDougall, much interest was taken in their utterances as indicative of the power of the Christian truth. Chief Pakan, of Whitefish Lake, felt keenly the loss of H. B. Steinhauer, who had died a short time before the uprising of the Indians, and whilst mourning the departure of his friend, the Cree Indians revolted.

Loyal and brave he remained, although some of Chief Big Bear's men sought to tamper with his young men. When referring to these times, during his visit to the east, he said: "As nearly as I can learn, I am now forty-six years of age, therefore I date beyond the incoming of the first missionary; and even after he came, I was distant from him, and only heard by rumor of his having come. Therefore, I saw much evil; I was with my people, far away in heathenism, and in everything that was wrong. Later the missionary reached our camp, and a change began to be apparent; and by-and-by, though wild, and stubborn, and wicked, the change affected me, Jesus Christ touched my heart, and I also embraced His religion; and I have made Him my Chief from that day unto this. I owe a great debt of gratitude to my old missionary, who recently left us, Mr. Steinhauer; he and other missionaries have done me great good, and have also done a great and grand work for my people. Later on, my people asked me to stand up for them, and I became their chief. They said, 'Try and help us on, and do not set any foolish example.' Last spring an opportunity came; we were approached with guns, and asked to take up our guns against the white man; we were dared not to do so; but I said in my heart, I want to keep his law, as I have embraced the law of the God he worships. I shall not go with you, nor shall any of my people. My people want to improve; I feel we have improved wondrously. We want to be like the white people, and make progress in civilization, and that which shall be everlasting in its benefit. As I feel that you are my friends, in listening to me as I speak, and in welcoming me as I come before you, I ask you still to be my friends, that not my band only, but my whole nation may rise in the scale of civilization and Christianity."

The zeal manifested by the Indians in the cause of Christ is great, when we consider their ancestry, native religious ideas and customs, and the numerous difficulties attending labor in that land. East and west, and far in the frozen north, the influence of the devoted Evans has spread, until missions have been established by the churches, and missionaries and teachers have gone among the lodges and erected school-houses and places for worship, where young and old may study the works and words of God, through the simple method devised by this sainted man.

He has gone from us; but his work is enduring and his record on high.

FINIS.

17

CPSIA information can be obtained at www.ICGtesting.com
Printed in the USA
LVOW051720210212

269754LV00016B/204/P